Michael P. O'Connor is a long-time Old West enthusiast and author of *The Wild West Meets the Big Apple*. He is a member of the Alamo Society, the Wild West History Association, and the Western Writers of America. He is a former U.S. Air Force officer. He has earned a bachelor's degree from Manhattan College and a Juris Doctor from St. John's University School of Law. O'Connor has been a practicing attorney for over thirty years and he, and his wife, Elise, currently divide their time between Cornwall, New York, and Pompano Beach, Florida.

This book is dedicated to Elise, Patrick, Cassie, Finley, Bailey, Margie, Kevin, Liam, Owen, and Sean. Love you all.

Michael P. O'Connor

THE TOP TEN HISTORICAL LOCATIONS OF THE OLD WEST

An Entertaining Narrative and Guide

AUSTIN MACAULEY PUBLISHERS™

LONDON • CAMBRIDGE • NEW YORK • SHARJAH

Ordering Information
Quantity sales: Special discounts are available on quantity purchases by corporations, associations, and others. For details, contact the publisher at the address below.

Publisher's Cataloging-in-Publication data
O'Connor, Michael P.
The Top Ten Historical Locations of the Old West

ISBN 9798889109280 (Paperback)
ISBN 9798889109297 (ePub e-book)

Library of Congress Control Number: 2023921407

www.austinmacauley.com/us

First Published 2024
Austin Macauley Publishers LLC
40 Wall Street, 33rd Floor, Suite 3302
New York, NY 10005
USA

mail-usa@austinmacauley.com
+1 (646) 5125767

A tip of the cowboy hat to Christopher Rosenbluth for his precise editing; Rachel Santino of Armadillo Proofreading for her professional formatting; Cassandra O'Connor and Julie Witmer for their map making skills; Eliot Linzer for his meticulous indexing.

Table of Contents

Introduction

The West. The Wild West. The hundred years in which the United States spanned from sea to sea through the efforts of hearty and determined Americans willing to overcome immeasurable obstacles to pursue what would become known as the American Dream. The traits required to settle the untamed Western wilderness—bravery, fortitude, toughness, and self-reliance—would come to define the American character.

The published journals of Lewis and Clark evolved into dime novels and twentieth-century movies and television dramas in which the real-life participants in our Western expansion became the embodiment of those admirable frontier qualities.

The dramatic exploits of Lewis and Clark, Davy Crockett, Wyatt Earp, Wild Bill Hickok, Jesse James, Billy the Kid, George Armstrong Custer, Sitting Bull, and Crazy Horse, although sensationalized and sanitized, did, in fact, occur. Which brings us to the point of this book. Where did the pivotal moments of the country's Western expansion occur?

As difficult as it was, like the title says, the historical locations have been narrowed down to ten: Northwest Pacific Coast, Mouth of the Columbia River between Washington and Oregon (the site where Lewis and Clark reached the Pacific Ocean); the Alamo, San Antonio, Texas; Marshall Park Gold Discovery State Historic Park, Coloma, California; Little Bighorn Valley, Montana; Deadwood, South Dakota; Dodge City, Kansas; St. Joseph, Missouri; Lincoln, New Mexico; Tombstone, Arizona; and Wounded Knee, Dakota Pine Ridge Indian Reservation, South Dakota.

Each chapter examines a location and not only describes the crucial event and its main participants but also analyzes the causes that lead to the climactic incident. Specifically, in the 'What Happened Here?' section, the reader is given not only a detailed account of the event's nuts and bolts but also its historical significance in shaping the history and legacy of the Old West. For example, a mere week after James Marshall found speckles of gold in the trace of Sutter's Mill, the Treaty of Guadalupe was signed, awarding to the United States the sleepy Mexican province of California. Within a year, California was granted statehood, upsetting the tenuous balance of free and slave states, and propelling the country closer to Civil War.

In the 'What Happened Next?' section of each chapter, the reader is given a history of the location since the pivotal event, such as the economic ups and downs of Tombstone resulting from devastating fires, and the inauspicious history of the revered Alamo Chapel, which even served as a grocery warehouse and was nearly torn down. What was thought to be tragic grass fires on the Little Bighorn Battlefield in 1983 turned out to be a bonanza for archaeologists who ultimately recovered over five thousand artifacts from the newly exposed surface.

The 'What Do I Do When I Get There?' section utilizes maps and then-and-now photographs to point the reader to available tours and museums with particular attention paid to surviving structures from the nineteenth century.

However, this is not a typical dry, sugarcoated guidebook. For example, the reader may be disappointed to learn that Dodge City's infamous Front Street is a recreation not even located on the original footprint, but the initial disappointment is overshadowed by the spectacular Boot Hill Museum. Similarly, a trip to Tombstone requires visiting the notorious Bird Cage Theater, which has stood since 1882 and probably marks the last time it was cleaned. It must be the dirtiest museum in North America, but it is chock-full of interesting artifacts (e.g., Bat Masterson's stirrup).

No journey to an Old West location is truly complete without imbibing at an authentic saloon. In the 'Where Can I Wet My Whistle?' section, the reader will benefit from my years of extensive research on the subject and be steered to colorful drinking establishments that served, or in many instances overserved, legendary Western personalities. Among the famous taverns described is Big Nose Kate in Tombstone, located on the site of the former Grand Hotel and a hangout of the Earps and Doc Holiday. Although the Grand Hotel did not survive the fire of 1882, fortunately, the bar did! Of course, when in Deadwood, a libation at Saloon #10, where Wild Bill Hickok played his last hand of cards, is mandatory. By the way, Deadwood has two Saloon #10s. You'll have to read the chapter to hear that story.

'What about Grub?' details culinary options for tourists, once again emphasizing surviving establishments from frontier days. For example, when exploring Northern California's gold rush country, Old Sacramento is home to several century-old eating establishments, including The Firehouse Restaurant, serving basic American fare in a circa 1853 firehouse. While on the Lewis and Clark trail in Astoria, Oregon, try the roasted turkey at Huber's Café, which has been serving customers since 1879.

'Where Can I Hang My Hat and Put My Boots under a Bed?' suggests lodging options that, in most instances, allow visitors to experience the same accommodations as their traveling predecessors a century before. For instance, Buffalo, Wyoming, a good jumping-off point for Little Bighorn country, is home to the Occidental Hotel. Its who's who of former guests include Tom Horn, Calamity Jane, and Butch Cassidy and the Sundance Kid. From a barstool at San Antonio's Menger Hotel, you can see the walls of the Alamo and stay where Teddy Roosevelt, Robert E. Lee, and even John Wayne stayed!

'What Should I Watch and Read Before I Hit the Trail?' recommends books and movies that deal with the historic venue and its main characters. You can't visit the Alamo without viewing John Wayne's classic 1960 blockbuster or walk along Dodge City's Front Street without reading Tom Clavin's 2016 bestseller.

Through first-hand knowledge, 'Tips from the Trail' gives down-to-earth advice on touring the locale, practical information like the best times to visit, and suggested itineraries. For example, in visiting Lewis and Clark country in Oregon and Washington, the funky beach town of Seaside, Washington, is a convenient and fun base of operations.

I visited every site mentioned in the book. Every single one. Every museum, saloon, hotel, restaurant, and saloon (did I say that twice?). As you can imagine, it took years putting cowboy boots on the ground. It was a labor of love. It is my sincere hope you get the opportunity to visit some (if not all) of these locales in which history was made.

WASHINGTON
Dismal Nitch
Lewis and Clark End of the Trail
OREGON
IDAHO
MONTANA
NORTH DAKOTA
MINNESOTA
Little Bighorn Valley
SOUTH DAKOTA
Deadwood
WYOMING
Wounded Knee
IOWA
Coloma
NEBRASKA
NEVADA
UTAH
St. Joseph
COLORADO
KANSAS
MISSOURI
CALIFORNIA
Dodge City
NEW MEXICO
OKLAHOMA
ARIZONA
Lincoln
Tombstone
TEXAS
San Antonio

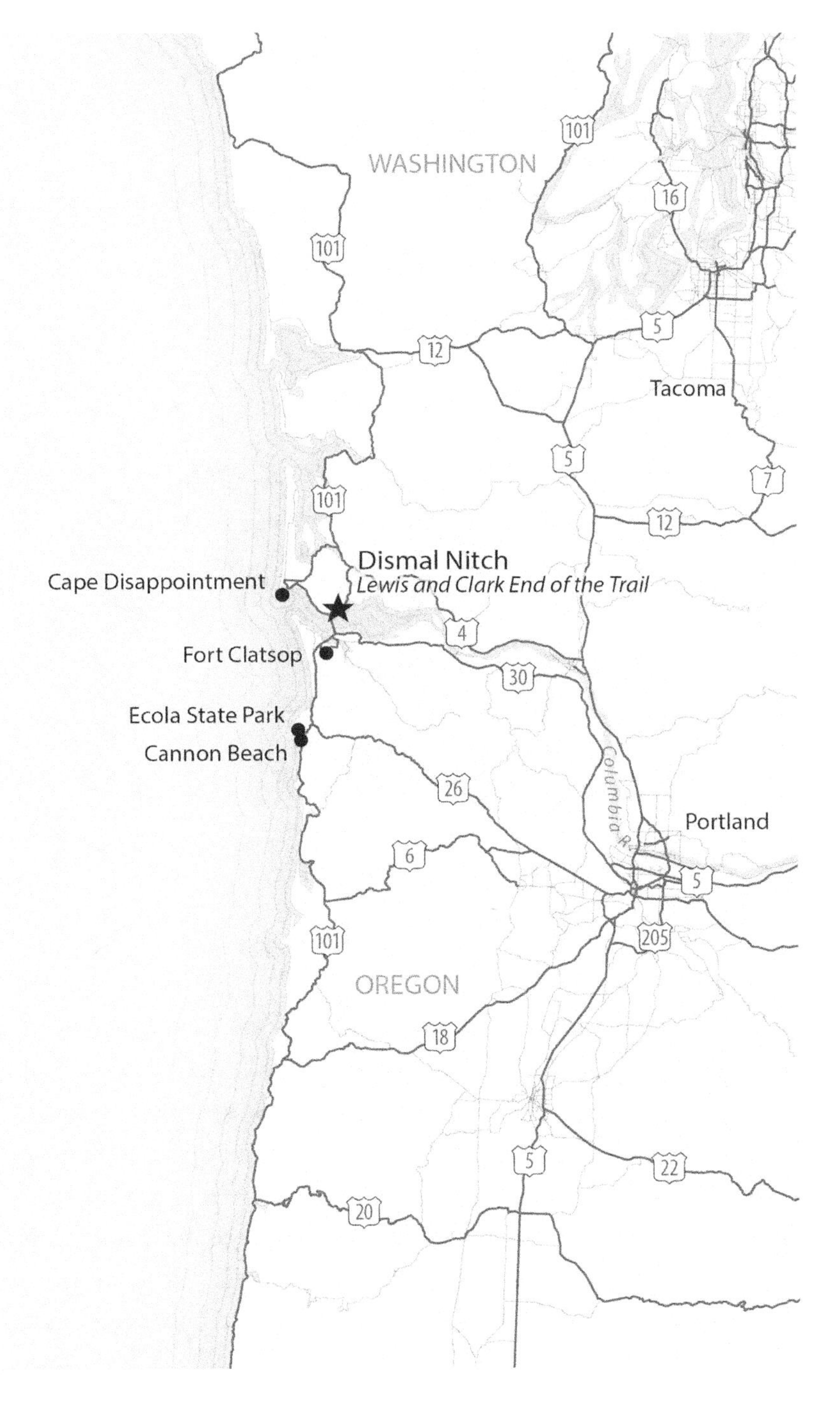

WASHINGTON
Tacoma
101
16
101
12
5
5
7
12
Cape Disappointment
Dismal Nitch
Lewis and Clark End of the Trail
4
30
Fort Clatsop
Ecola State Park
Cannon Beach
26
6
Columbia R.
Portland
5
205
101
OREGON
18
5
22
20

Northwest Pacific Coast, Mouth of the Columbia River

Washington and Oregon

Captains Lewis and Clark (National Archives)

WHAT HAPPENED HERE?

On November 7, 1805, after traversing nearly four thousand miles in over a year and a half, Captains Meriwether Lewis and William Clark and their Corps of Discovery thought they'd finally reached their ultimate destination: The Pacific Ocean. Clark, weary from the harrowing expedition and desperate for its end, believed his ears could hear the Pacific's crashing waves and even believed his eyes could see through the sporadically lifting fog the ebb and flow of its powerful tide. His heartfelt cheer, which he recorded in his field notes, drips with the elation he felt at that moment: "Ocian in view! O! The joy!"

But the ever-optimistic explorer was still twenty miles from the ocean. What he saw there between present-day Washington and Oregon was actually an estuary of the Columbia River, which he and his team viewed from the

Washington side at Point Ellice, a place they would appropriately name 'Dismal Nitch'. With the weather worsening, Lewis and Clark made the spot their expedition's final campsite. It would be another eight days before the Corps' canoes could get around the cove. Finally, on November 15, the weary but excited explorers cast their eyes on the Pacific Ocean, their hard-earned goal finally before them.

Exploring the continent from the Mississippi River to the Pacific had been for decades a passion of President Thomas Jefferson. Jefferson had foreseen that America's destiny lay in the West. Decades before the coining of the term 'Manifest Destiny', the Sage of Monticello recognized that for the United States not only to prosper but to survive, it needed to possess the entire continent, from the Atlantic to the Pacific. By the dawn of the nineteenth century, the reign of the old European powers was coming to an end, and the vast expanse of fertile land spanning the continent was ripe for the taking. But, first, it had to be explored.

Fittingly, on July 4, 1803, Jefferson announced to the young nation that he had just sealed the deal with Napoleon's France on the Louisiana Purchase. For fifteen million dollars, the United States had doubled in size, acquiring eight hundred twenty-five thousand square miles, stretching west from the Mississippi River and east of the Continental Divide. That same day, the president issued his orders to Captain Meriwether Lewis to command the Corps of Discovery to explore the Missouri River westward "by its course and communication with the waters of the Pacific Ocean, whether the Columbia, Oregon, Colorado, or any other river, may offer the most direct and practicable water communication across this continent for the purposes of commerce." In other words, the Corps of Discovery was commissioned to find the fabled Northwest Passage: an all-water route across the continent, linking the Atlantic and Pacific, facilitating trade with the Orient.

Thomas Jefferson
(National Archives)

Jefferson and Lewis had been meticulously planning the expedition for years, pouring over maps and meeting with the world's leading botanists, doctors, and scientists. The president had handpicked Lewis, who was his former personal secretary and military officer, as well as an old family friend and Virginia neighbor. In turn, the twenty-nine-year-old Lewis handpicked his co-commander, the thirty-three-year-old William Clark, also an army officer. Although Clark's commission would not be approved until an Act of Congress posthumously recognized it almost two hundred years later, he was nonetheless considered the exploration's co-commander and addressed as captain by the men serving under him.

The Corps consisted of approximately thirty volunteer soldiers, a few hired civilians, Clark's slave, York, and Lewis's Newfoundland dog, Seaman. It left St. Louis on May 14, 1804, facing a daunting and unprecedented task. In addition to paddling over two thousand miles up Missouri and lugging two tons of equipment and supplies, which included a hundred fifty gallons of whiskey, they were to map the uncharted territory, assess its natural resources, collect samples of native animals and fauna, and, hopefully, befriend any Indians they encountered. And, then, of course, they had to retrace their path and return.

William Clark
(Reproduction of watercolor
by Charles Wilson Peale,
Billings Public Library)

It had been anticipated that they would find an easy portage that would connect the Missouri River, which drains east, with the Columbia River, which drains West. They soon found that was not the case. The Corps faced swift rapids, particularly on the upper Missouri, which forced them to walk the route, carrying, or, in some cases, abandoning their canoes. What they thought was a 'ridge of hills' on the Continental Divide turned out to be the imposing Bitterroot Mountains of present-day Montana, which took them weeks to cross. In addition to the formidable physical obstacles, historians estimate Lewis and Clark encountered over fifty different Indian tribes, each with their own unique language and customs. It is a credit to the leaders' resourcefulness and diplomacy skills that during the entire round trip, a journey that took three years and covered eight thousand miles, only two Indians were killed and one expedition member lost due to illness. Perhaps the most fortuitous occurrence

of the entire journey occurred on November 4, 1804. While camped on the
banks of the Missouri River in what is now
North Dakota, a French-Canadian trapper
named Toussaint Charbonneau walked into
their camp and offered himself as an
interpreter. He also offered the services of
one of his wives, a fifteen-year-old
Shoshone who had been captured four
years earlier by a rival tribe and 'rescued'
when Charbonneau won her in a bet with
her captors. The teenager's name was
Sacagawea, and she would prove to be an
invaluable asset to Lewis and Clark, aiding
them in communicating and, most
importantly, trading with the tribes they

Meriweather Lewis, 1805, by
Charles Balthazar Julien Fevret de
Saint-Memin (National Portraits)

would encounter for desperately needed essentials, such as food and horses.
Captain Clark would later reflect that Sacagawea's efforts on "that long
dangerous and fatiguing rout to the Pacific Ocian and back deserved a greater
reward for her attention and services on that route than we had in our power to
give her."

Charbonneau did not fare as well in the estimation of the captains. Lewis
characterized him as "a man of no particular merit." He did provide vital
services as an interpreter, however, being familiar with some Indian languages.
The interpreting process worked like the old game of telephone line: Sacagawea
would translate to Charbonneau, who would then translate the phrase into
French, so a Corps member who spoke both French and English could speak
to Captains Lewis and Clark. Whatever the process, it worked.

As if she didn't have enough to do, Sacagawea, who was pregnant at the
time she and her husband joined the expedition, gave birth to a healthy boy,

Jean Baptiste Charbonneau, nicknamed 'Pompey', while the team was en route to the Pacific. Clark oversaw the delivery.

Midwifery was not the only medical service provided by Clark on the expedition. Prior to the journey, Clark had consulted

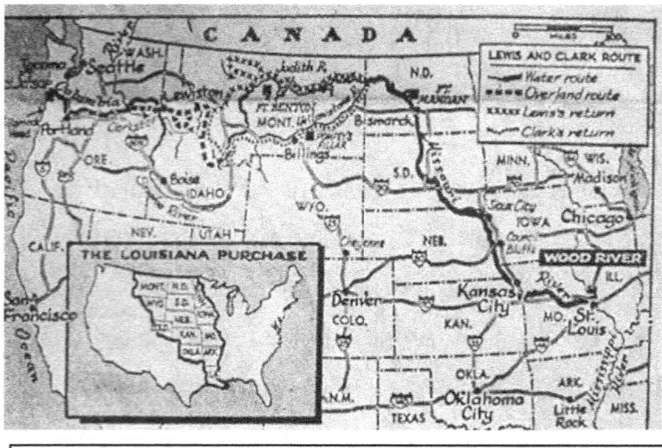

Lewis and Clark Map (Ft. Clatsop Collection)

with Dr. Benjamin Rush, the leading physician of the day. Over the course of the trip, Clark was called upon to treat various ailments, big and small, of not only the Corps members but also of unwell Indians they encountered along the way. The cornerstone of Clark's treatment regimen was 'Rush's Bilious Pills', an explosive laxative touted to be a miraculous cure-all.

Clark liberally dispensed the purging 'thunder clappers' to treat a wide range of afflictions, from malaria to dysentery, with predictable results. Clark also used his wonder drug to treat what would become a common ailment for the Corps: syphilis. Yes, syphilis. Perhaps surprisingly to Lewis and Clark, the men of the tribes they encountered proved willing, even eager, to allow their wives to engage in amorous relations with the explorers. It was a common belief among the Indians that the apparent power of the strange newcomers could be absorbed through sexual interaction. Clark noted in his journal that the "squares… were very fond of caressing our men."

York, who the natives nicknamed 'the big Medison', proved to be particularly popular among the Indian maidens. Whether any mystical attributes were passed along is lost to history, but what is not lost is the fact that most, if not all, of the Corps' members contracted the dreaded venereal disease, which had spread to the tribes through contact with early European trappers. The common treatment for syphilis, well into the twentieth century, was mercury, of which Clark had plenty and dispensed generously. Because mercury does not decompose in the soil, archaeologists have been able to uncover the specific locations of some of the expedition's campsites by detecting mercury in old latrine pits.

In early November 1805, after over six hundred miles of water travel on the Clearwater, Snake, and Columbia Rivers, the Corps of Discovery was finally within sight of the Pacific. On November 10, the Corps camped on the northern side of the Columbia, at Point Ellice, in a cove surrounded by steep, jagged cliffs. For the next five days, they were essentially pinned down by rain, strong winds, and rising tides.

On November 15, the weather finally broke, and the miserable, soaked explorers were able to navigate around Pont Ellice. They established a temporary camp, unceremoniously dubbed Station Camp, which would serve as a base of operations for the next ten days, during which the Corps members excitedly explored the surroundings of the Pacific Coast.

While at Station Camp, Captain Clark and ten men hiked about a dozen miles to the end of the Long Beach Peninsula, where the mouth of the Columbia meets the Pacific at a place called Cape Disappointment. Clark had hoped to spot from the high cliffs 

Cape Disappointment

overlooking the ocean European ships that might offer them transport back east. Unfortunately, no such vessels could be seen. While this was surely upsetting, it was not the event that gave the location its name. Cape Disappointment had earned its moniker over a decade prior. In 1788, a British sea Captain, searching for the 'great river of the West', had somewhat inexplicably mistaken the mouth of the Columbia for a bay. Hence the name.

The weather was getting colder, and the Corps had to decide where to hunker down for the winter. The co-commanders decided to do something uniquely American: they put the decision to a vote of all the Corps members, including not just the Corps members but also Sacagawea and York. In addition to being the first vote ever held in the Pacific Northwest, it was also the first time either a black slave or a woman was allowed to vote. The winning choice was 

Fort Clatsop (Fort Clatsop Collection)

to cross the Columbia and explore the river's south (Oregon) side for a suitable location.

On the south side of the Columbia, the local Clatsop Indian tribe had indicated that game was plentiful in the area that is now Oregon, and the captains ultimately found a 'most eligible' site a couple of miles up the Lewis and Clark River. It was on a high bluff with plenty of trees that could be used for building their winter quarters. The spot had an added bonus in that it was only a few miles from the ocean that allowed them to make salt and keep a watchful eye out for any ships.

The men immediately started construction on their winter camp, which they named Fort Clatsop, in honor of the local tribe that had been so helpful. The structures, which took over three weeks to complete, were finished by the end of the year. The cramped quarters, a pair of log structures facing each other surrounded by palisade walls enclosing a fifty square foot area, would serve as the Corps' home for the next three months.

During the winter, the men had daily contact with the local Clatsop and Chinook Indians with the enlisted men doing their best to spread their attributes to natives. All was not fun and games, however. The cold weather was depressing, and in addition to making salt, the men kept busy by hunting and tediously scraping and tanning elk hides to make moccasins.

Beached Whale (Ft. Clatsop Collection)

A welcome diversion occurred in late December when a whale washed ashore at what is now the resort area of Cannon Beach. Clark and some Corps members took the six-mile hike. Sacagawea, who insisted on seeing 'that monstrous fish', went along as well. By the time they arrived at the beach, all that remained was the skeleton, whose length of a hundred-and-five feet Captain Clark promptly measured and recorded.

On March 23, 1806, the Corps, as noted by Lewis, "bid final adieu to Fort Clatsop." Unfortunately for the travel-worn company, there would be no ship to take them back to civilization, and so they began their treacherous four-thousand-mile journey back to St. Louis.

The expedition made it back to St. Louis six months later on September 23, 1806. They made much better time, for not only were they familiar with the route but they did not have to draw maps and collect specimens. The return trip was not without incident, however: a nearsighted Corpsmen with one eye, taking aim at an elk, accidentally shot Lewis in the buttocks. In true military fashion, the visually impaired private denied culpability and claimed it must have been an Indian. While Lewis, who would fully recover from his painful wound, did not believe him, he nevertheless let the incident go.

Immediately upon arriving, Lewis began writing a report to President Jefferson, the first communication to the president in a year and a half. There was much to report.

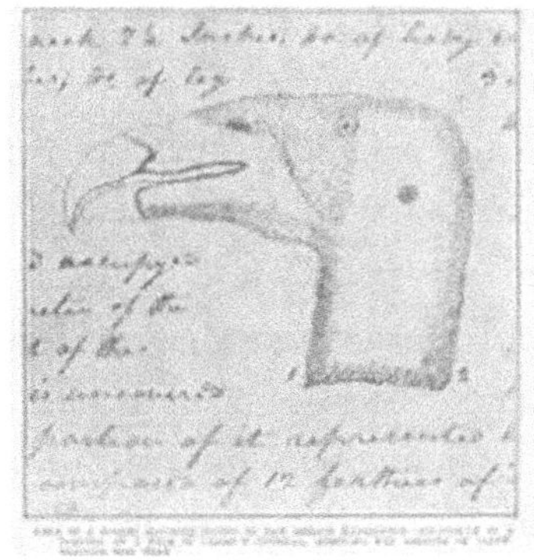

Clark's Journal (Fort Clatsop Collection)

Although it was clearly disappointing that an all-water route did not exist, Lewis and Clark had successfully mapped the most direct route across the continent. Additionally, they had discovered and accurately recorded hundreds of previously undiscovered plants and animal species. In addition to Clark

making intricate sketches of animals and birds, he collected numerous animal hides, horns, and bird skins and even shipped a live prairie dog back to Jefferson.

Lewis, right away, started working on publishing his and Clark's journals. Upon returning to Washington, Lewis and Jefferson lobbied various politicians for compensation for the Corps members. After much wrangling, each man received double pay. Lewis and Clark were each granted sixteen hundred acres of land, and each enlisted man received three hundred twenty acres. Meanwhile, Sacagawea and York, who remained a slave despite pleading with Clark to grant him his freedom, would receive no compensation for their service. Years later, after Sacagawea's death of an unknown illness in 1814, Clark would adopt Pompey and his sister, Lizzette.

Lewis savored his newfound celebrity status in Washington, particularly enjoying the dinner circuit and perhaps drinking too much. In 1807, his mentor appointed him governor of the Louisiana Territory and dispatched him back out West. But Lewis was a man of action and proved to be ill-suited for the governmental duties required to oversee the vast territory. He was further distracted by his futile attempts to get his journals published, which wouldn't happen until 1814, five years after he died a violent and mysterious death on October 11, 1809 (see p. 33). Neither his nor Clark's estates would ever receive a penny from their sale.

Despite the disappointments of the publishing industry, Clark fared much better in later life than his ill-fated co-commander. He married in 1808. A year later, he would christen his first-born son Meriwether Lewis Clark in homage to his friend. He also embarked on a successful political career, serving as governor of the Missouri Territory and superintendent of Indian Affairs. He died in 1838 of natural causes at the age of sixty-eight.

In addition to the detailed maps, animal and plant specimens, and inroads on Indian relations, the Corps of Discovery opened the West to Americans, almost immediately. The United States would not be denied; it would stretch from sea to shining sea. In 1846, when the United States, through the Oregon Treaty, acquired all the land west of the Rockies to the Pacific, one of the reasons cited by the United States for its entitlement to the vast territory was the exploration by Lewis and Clark four decades earlier.

Columbia River

In the ensuing centuries, the tumultuous Columbia River navigated by Lewis and Clark has been tamed by numerous dams and locks, making it much more navigable than when the Corps of Discovery traveled it. Today, the Columbia River, from its mouth at the Pacific Ocean to the vast canyons of the Columbia River Gorge, is a mecca for all types of outdoor water recreation.

WHAT DO I DO WHEN I GET THERE?

Lewis and Clark National Historical Park, Oregon and Washington

This joint venture between the National Park Service and the states of Washington and Oregon encompasses twelve different sites and rings around the mouth of the Columbia River and the Pacific Coast for forty miles. The

State and National Park sites focus on Lewis and Clark and the Corps of Discovery's activities during the winter of 1805–1806, as well as the history of Chinook and Clatsop Indians, who called this region home for thousands of years.

OREGON:

Fort Clatsop Replica & Visitor Center, 92343 Fort Clatsop Road, Astoria, Oregon, (503)861-2471

Inside the Fort Clatsop Visitor Center, visitors can view two films and explore exhibits and artifacts associated with the Corps' experiences on the Pacific Coast. A short walk brings you to the replica fort, where reenactors describe the everyday toils faced by the expedition members in the winter of 1805–1806. The fort was reconstructed in 1955, and it is a little disappointing that historians and archaeologists haven't pinpointed the exact location of the winter quarters. But it's close enough.

Ft. Clatsop

Fort to Sea Trail, Oregon

A six-and-a-half-mile trail from Fort Clatsop to Sunset Beach mirrors the trek the explorers took to the ocean. The problem is you have to walk back. Another option is to drive five miles south on Highway 101 to the Sunset Beach trailhead and walk about half a mile to the beach. Worked for me.

Ecola State Park, Oregon

Within the park lie various trails focusing on the spectacular views of the rugged Oregon Pacific Coast. The literature on the park is a little confusing because it implies you can hike a marked trail to the beach where Clark and other Corps members, including Sacagawea, hiked to gaze upon the remains of the beached whale. You can't. The actual site is on present-day Cannon Beach, close to the imposing Haystack Rock, which is not encompassed in Ecola State Park.

If you desire to tread on the beach where the infamous whale carcass was viewed by the astonished explorers, you have to drive south from the park to Cannon Beach, which is a bustling summer beach town. Without a doubt, Captain Clark got there more easily than I did, and I know for sure he didn't get a parking ticket. It is also a little tricky to find access to the beach. You can see it; you just can't get there. Kind of like driving in New Jersey.

Lesson learned: People with million-dollar homes overlooking the beach do not like strangers traipsing through their backyard trying to get to the beach.

Cannon Beach

In fairness to them, though, they are probably tired of tourists asking them where the beached whale site is located (only kidding—nobody had any idea what I was talking about). There are no markers commemorating the site, but you can use your imagination, using the distinctive Haystack Rock as a guidepost.

The Salt Works, Lewis and Clark Way, Seaside, Oregon

The beach where the Corps built a furnace to produce the desperately needed salt to replenish the supply that had run out of by the time they reached the Pacific. The site is a recreated oven, replicating those used by the explorers to boil the ocean water to extract its salt. To my surprise, it is not located on the beach, but a couple of blocks away in what

Salt works

appears to be somebody's backyard. The story goes that in 1900 a descendant of a Clatsop remembered the location of the site, and the property was ultimately donated to a historical society.

WASHINGTON

Cape Disappointment State Park, 244 Robert Gray Drive, Ilwaco, Washington

Situated at the mouth of the Columbia River, this is where the Corps of Discovery first viewed the Pacific Ocean. The Lewis and Clark Interpretive Center outlines their trials and triumphs

Salt Works

Cape Disappointment Museum

through exhibits, artifacts, and pictures. There is an interpretive center, which has a museum that is actually quite good. Sadly, few artifacts from the expedition remain, since, when the Corps returned to St. Louis, many of the items that survived the voyage, such as rifles, utensils, and powder horns, were auctioned off to raise money for advances on payments due to the men. One of the museum's pleasant surprises was a display of artifacts, such as a flask and a hatchet, once belonging to Sgt. Patrick Gass the last surviving member of the Corps of Discovery, who passed away in 1870 at the ripe old age of ninety-eight. The park has also some well-marked hiking trails, all with breathtaking views of the Columbia and Pacific, the same sites Captain Clark enjoyed over two hundred years ago.

Station Camp, 354 US 101, Chinook, Washington

The encampment where the Corps of Discovery spent ten days and got its first real glimpse of the Pacific Ocean is

Station Camp

marked by a small sign, right off the highway. Be alert because you can drive right past it. It is a little underwhelming. It has some informational markers, mostly about the Chinook Indians and local fauna, as well as a few replica canoes.

Dismal Nitch, 230 Route 401, Chinook, Washington

A couple miles north of station camp (US 101 turns into Route 401) is a rest area marked by a 'Dismal Nitch' sign. The pullout has a historical marker describing the horrible weather the Corps endured for six days. It is interesting because you can gaze down the cliffs into the cove and visualize the precarious position the expedition had gotten itself into, pinned against the jagged rocks. You can also see Point Ellice, which blocked the explorers' view of the Pacific.

IS THERE ANYTHING ELSE?

End of the Oregon Trail Interpretive and Visitor Center, 1726 Washington St., Oregon City, Oregon

Interactive displays and reenactors explore the history of the Oregon Trail, which guided over five hundred thousand pioneers on a two thousand-mile journey to Oregon City.

Fort Stevens State Park, 100 Peter Iredale Rd., Hammond, Oregon

Once home to the Clatsop Indians, the fort was an active military installation from the Civil War through World War II. Today, the four-thousand-and-three-hundred-acre park is a haven for camping, hiking, and biking. From the park's observation deck, one can view the mouth of the mighty Columbia River as it meets the Pacific.

Oregon Historical Museum, 1200 SW Park Ave., Portland, Oregon (503)222-1741 (orhist@ohs.org)

The museum's prized possession is the branding iron used by Captain Lewis to scorch his name onto a tree near station camp on the north side of the

Columbia River in Washington. The remarkable artifact was uncovered in 1890 on one of the islands above the Long Narrows on the Columbia. Spoiler alert: It is not always on display. However, in the obligatory gift shop, you can purchase a replica for sixty dollars. Even without the showpiece, the museum is worth visiting.

It displays artifacts from the Native Americans that lived on the Columbia plateau for centuries, as well as clothes and cooking utensils from the Oregon Trail period, from 1840 until 1860, when almost a half million pilgrims made their way to Oregon. The institution also periodically hosts temporary exhibitions on such sundry topics as the Beatles and Oregon ballet. I don't know. The branding iron would have been cool if it were displayed.

Riverview Cemetery, 0300 SW Taylors Ferry Road, Portland, Oregon, the Final Resting Place of Virgil Earp
ASTORIA:

Founded by John Jacob Astor, it is the oldest North American settlement west of the Rocky Mountains. This picturesque coastal town hosts the Columbia River Maritime Museum, the Flavel House Museum (441 8th Street), and a vibrant historic downtown district. From the century-old Astoria Column (1 Coxcomb Drive), visitors have unsurpassed views of the scenic Northwest Pacific Coast. You can also purchase a lightweight, wooden plane that you can throw from the tower. On the grounds, a historical marker outlines Clark's first view of the ocean.

Astoria Column

WHERE CAN I WET MY WHISTLE?

Deschutes Brewery, 210 NW 11th Ave., Portland, Oregon

There is no shortage of microbreweries in Oregon, but this one is particularly good. Try the Fresh Squeezed IPA.

Buoy Beer, 18th St., Astoria, Oregon

Situated on an old pier on the Columbia River, it's a great location, complete with a partial glass floor, allowing you to view seals frolicking (and sleeping) under the pier.

Portway Tavern, 422 W. Marine Dr., Astoria, OR 97103, (503)325-2651 (theportway.com)

The self-proclaimed oldest watering hole in the oldest settlement west of the Rockies (although the sign proudly declares it was established in 1923). A cozy dive (that's a compliment) tastefully decorated with orange life preservers.

WHAT ABOUT GRUB?

Huber's Café, 411 SW 3rd Ave., Portland, OR 97204, (503)228-5686 (hubers.com)

Established in 1879 and in its present location since 1910, it is Portland's oldest restaurant. Serving up American fare, its signature plate is the roasted turkey. The flamboyantly served, potent Spanish coffee is a must.

Dundee's Bar & Grill, 414 Broadway, Seaside, Oregon

Located in the middle of the beach-type establishments, it has a friendly spacious bar and great burgers.

WHERE CAN I HANG MY HAT AND PUT MY BOOTS UNDER A BED?

SEASIDE

Seaside, Oregon, is a convenient location for traveling to the Lewis and Clark sites. It's a beach town, so there are a lot of touristy, beach attractions in town, although not many people are on the beach (I don't know, I'm used to the Jersey shore). There are some typical motels that are serviceable (if you don't mind not having air-conditioning), but they're on the pricey side if you go during summer.

- Beachside Inn, 300 5th Ave., Seaside, Oregon, (800)845-1284
- Coast River Inn, 800 S. Holladay Dr., Seaside, Oregon, (503)738-8474
- If B&Bs are your thing: Gilbert Inn, 341 Beach Drive, Seaside, Oregon, (800)507–2714

PORTLAND

- Sentinel Hotel, 614 SW 11th Ave., Portland, OR 97205, (503)224-3400 (sentinel.com)—operating since 1909 and conveniently located near historic Pioneer Square, this luxury hotel is housed in two historic downtown buildings. It also houses a popular restaurant, Jake's Grill, with a great bar good for a late afternoon respite or a nightcap and the busy Jackknife Bar. It's quaint with lots of nooks and crannies.

WHAT SHOULD I WATCH AND READ BEFORE I HIT THE TRAIL?

BOOKS

- *Undaunted Courage* (1996, by Stephen E. Ambrose)—the seminal nonfiction work on Lewis and Clark by one of America's greatest historians
- *The Lewis and Clark Journals: An Epic of Discovery* (2004, edited by Gary E. Moulton)—an abridged version of the Lewis and Clark journals blended with observations made by enlisted men on the expedition

VIDEOS

- *The Far Horizon* (1955, Paramount DVD)—surprisingly, there is a dearth of films on the expedition, but Hollywood outdid itself with this feature. Fred McMurray is Lewis and Charlton Heston is Clark, who falls in love with Sacagawea, played by Donna Reed. Enough said.

- *Lewis and Clark* (1997, DVD, PBS Home Video)—the epic story of the Corp of Discovery as only Ken Burns can tell it
- *Lewis and Clark: Great Journey West* (2002, IMAX)—IMAX large-screen documentary examining the expedition

TIPS FROM THE TRAIL

You're going to spend a lot of time driving up and down Highway 101, and the stretch between Seaside and Cannon Beach is always congested. To hit all the Lewis and Clark sites will take two days or longer if you want to take advantage of some of the hiking trails. Your best bet is to hit the Washington sites one day and the Oregon sites on the other. Take it all in; the scenery is breathtaking. If you've been bitten by the Lewis and Clark bug, the National Park Service maintains the Lewis and Clark Trail, which extends almost five thousand miles through sixteen states. Check out their website (nps.gov) for maps and more info.

The Tragic and Mysterious Death of Meriwether Lewis

In the early morning hours of October 11, 1809, the thirty-five-year-old Lewis was found dead inside a wayside inn in Tennessee, the victim of two gunshot wounds. Lewis, who at the time was the governor of Louisiana, had been traveling from St. Louis to Washington to meet with government officials and to check on the progress of the publication of the expedition's most anticipated journals. He was riding with Chickasaw agent Major James Neelly and two free Black servants when they stopped for the night at Grinder's Inn, about seventy miles southwest of Nashville, along the well-traveled Natchez Trace.

Lewis had not been well. Earlier in the trip, while on a keelboat, he has been confined to his bed, possibly with malaria. Members of the keelboat crew would later recall that Lewis twice attempted to take his own life. Neelly would later confirm that Lewis "appeared at times deranged in mind."

Meriweather Lewis
Memorial (Lewis
County Tennessee)

When they arrived at the inn, on the evening of October 10, Neelly was not present, having gone off in search of two horses that had gotten loose.

Mrs. Grinder would recollect that Lewis had been acting strangely before retiring for the night. He preferred to sleep on the floor, rather than in an available bed, and was seen pacing back and forth, talking to himself. Before retiring for the night, Lewis had made an odd request for his servant to bring him gunpowder.

At 3:00 on the morning of the eleventh, Mrs. Grinder, who couldn't sleep because of Lewis's incoherent ramblings, heard two pistol shots. She saw Lewis stagger from his room and shout, "O madam! Give me some water and heal my wounds." When she finally summoned the courage to investigate, she was shocked to find Lewis stretched out on the floor, his brain exposed by a gunshot wound to the skull. He suffered another gaping hole in his chest. He then reportedly told his servant, "I have done the business, my good servant. Give me some water."

He further requested that the servant take his rifle and put him out of his misery, which the servant refused to do. The famous explorer's last words were, "I am no coward, but I am so strong, so hard to die." Major Neeley, Captain Clark, and Jefferson would all later surmise that Lewis had committed suicide, with Jefferson noting that Lewis was subject to 'sensible depressions of mind'.

Not everybody was convinced that Lewis took his own life, particularly Lewis's relatives. How could the expert marksman almost botch his own suicide? There was no shortage of suspects: roaming bandits on the infamously dangerous Natchez Trace? Major Neely? The servants? Mrs. Grinder? Perhaps even an enraged Mr. Grinder, who, upon finding his betrothed in a compromising position with the territorial governor, took fatal action?

The murder conspiracy got new life when, in the 1840s, a Tennessee commission exhumed Lewis's body to erect a monument over the grave. They took the opportunity to examine the body and noted, without explanation, that "it was more probable that he died at the hands of an assassin." Periodically,

Lewis's descendants request the National Park Service exhume the remains for an autopsy, but thus far, they have been unsuccessful. We may never know how the great explorer perished.

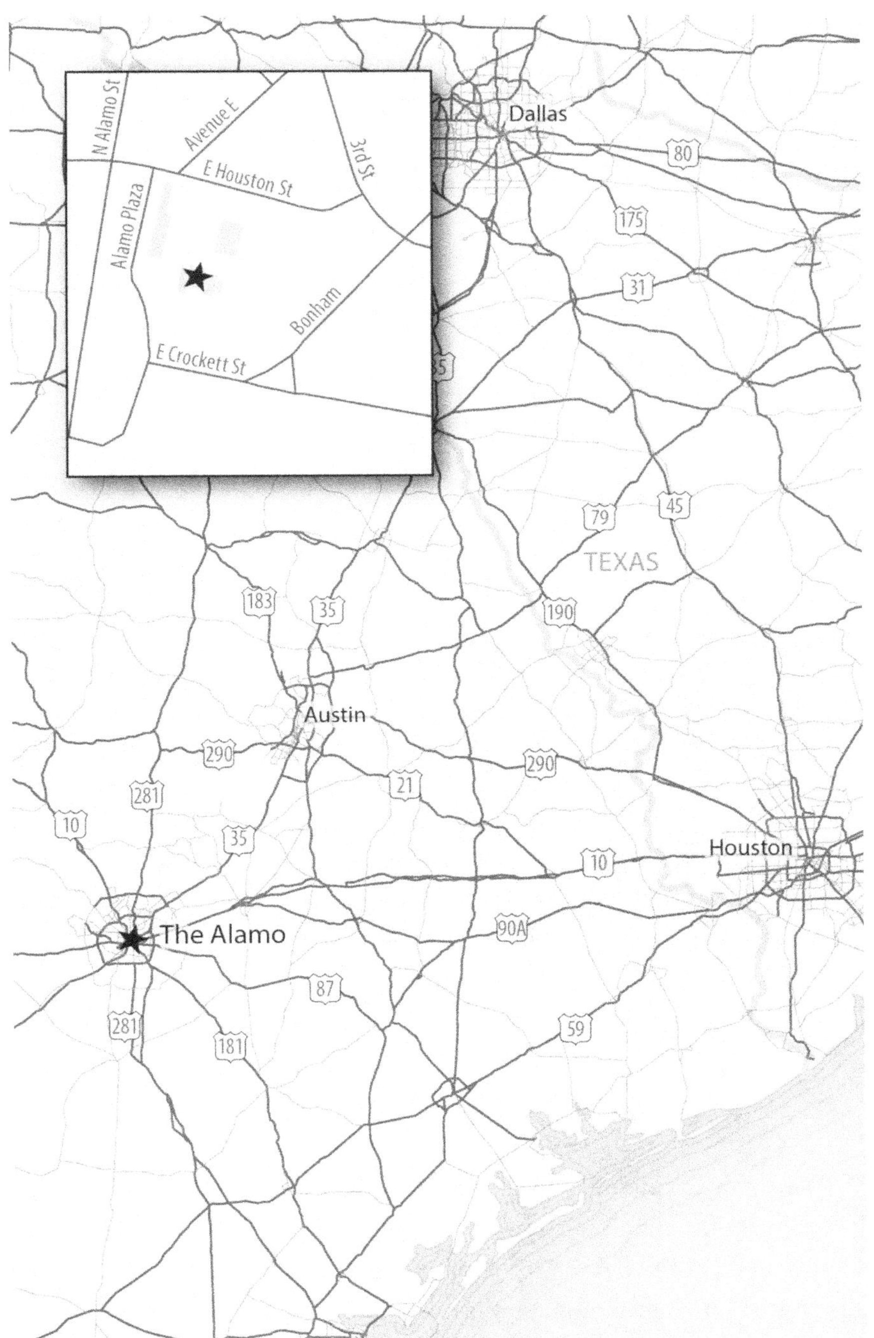

N Alamo St
Avenue E
E Houston St
3rd St
Alamo Plaza
Bonham
E Crockett St
Dallas
80
175
31
45
79
TEXAS
190
183
35
Austin
290
290
281
21
10
35
Houston
10
90A
The Alamo
87
281
59
181

The Alamo

San Antonio, Texas

The Alamo

WHAT HAPPENED HERE?

If you don't remember what happened here, you're reading the wrong book. By the time the sun rose over the cold south Texas plains on the morning of March 6, 1836, arguably the most heroic battle ever fought on the North American continent was over, approximately ninety minutes after it had begun. The Texians' defeat was total; all of the approximately two hundred volunteers lay dead within the dilapidated walls of the century-old Mission San Antonio de Valero, known as the Alamo. The gallant defenders of the old mission-turned-fortress, refusing to surrender, ultimately lost their thirteen-day struggle against a far superior Mexican force.

In historical retrospect, armed conflict between the Texians and the Mexican army was inevitable. Since 1821, the Mexican government had been attracting immigrants from the United States and Europe by offering land grants of four thousand four hundred and twenty-eight acres of free land to those resilient enough to settle in its most northern province. Initially, the arrangement was mutually beneficial, providing an opportunity for a fresh start for the immigrants, while establishing settlements in the sparsely populated harsh terrain of Texas. American settlers soon vastly outnumbered the Mexicans and Mexico City finally realized that it had let the fox in the henhouse. But Mexico had a new fox hunter on the horizon: General Antonio Lopez de Santa Anna.

In 1830, Mexico City instituted a new colonization law banning further immigration from the United States and otherwise restricting the Texan's rights as Mexican citizens. In 1835, Santa Anna appointed himself dictator and dispatched his brother-in-law General Martin Perfecto de Cos, and a thousand troops to enforce martial law in Texas. In response, the Texians began forming a militia and haphazardly preparing for war.

The unorganized Texians began calling for volunteers and concentrating their forces in San Antonio de Bexar, the largest town in the province.

General Cos arrived in San Antonio de Bexar and stationed his troops inside the sprawling Alamo compound, located just east of the town, across the San Antonio River. The mission had been built in 1718 by Spanish Franciscan friars attempting to spread the good word of Christianity to the Texas Indians, and over the next three decades, the complex was utilized as a Spanish-Mexican army garrison. One of the military outfits utilizing the mission off and on over the years was a company of Spanish Lancers from Alamo de Parras, Mexico, providing the origin of the mission's iconic nickname.

Cos' forces clashed with the Texians in the streets of Bexar, and, incredibly, after five days of fighting against three hundred Texian volunteers, on December 9, 1835, Cos surrendered. As was the military custom, at the time, the Texians allowed General Cos and his troops to return south over the Rio Grande upon their promise not to take up arms again against the Texians.

Cos kept his pledge until he ran into his unhappy brother-in-law, who was steadfastly trudging north, to quash the infant rebellion. Cos and his soldiers joined the march, swelling Santa Anna's ranks to as many as four thousand men.

Santa Anna arrived in San Antonio de Bexar on February 23, 1836, and immediately raised a blood-red flag in the tower of San Antonio's San Fernando Cathedral, signaling that no quarter would be given to the Alamo defenders.

Upon Santa Anna's grand entrance into San Antonio de Bexar, the Texians retreated into the Alamo compound. The defenders who found themselves inside the Alamo were a hearty group. They came from all walks of life and were determined to make a fresh start in Texas. Although they may have had varied backgrounds, they had a common desire to live free in a Republic, and they were not about to be subject to a dictatorship. The volunteers also consisted of native Mexicans, who had settled in Texas (Tejanos), and likewise were unwilling to subject themselves to the autocratic whims of any man. Among the defenders were three men, who would henceforth be recognized as the embodiment of the mixture of fact and myth that almost immediately was transformed into the legend of the heroic last stand of the battle of the Alamo: William Barret Travis, James Bowie, and David Crockett.

William Barret Travis sketch by Wyly Martin, the only known likeness of Travis drawn during his lifetime (National Archives)

The commander of the Alamo garrison was William Travis, an ambitious twenty-six-year-old lawyer from South Carolina. Leaving a failed marriage and a stack of debts behind, Travis arrived in Texas in 1831 and became a leading proponent of Texas independence. During the thirteen-day siege, Travis sent a number of dispatches seeking reinforcements and affirming the Texian's resolve to fight to the death.

His February 24 dispatch, in which he addresses 'the people of Texas & all Americans in the world', informs them "I shall never surrender or retreat," and concludes 'Victory or Death', is one of the most inspirational letters written in American history.

James Bowie, c. 1820,
the only known oil
painting of Bowie

Travis' initially shared command of the Alamo with James Bowie with Travis in charge of the Regulars and Bowie in command of the volunteers. The forty-year-old Bowie was already a famous man and one to be reckoned with. Bowie's fame evolved from his ability to come out on top of deadly knife fights along the perilous Mississippi River and from the twelve inches double-bladed, razor-sharp killing instrument that bore his name. The former slave trader and dubious land speculator had ventured to Texas in 1825, like other American adventurers, in search of land and Mexican silver. He prospered in Texas with some assistance from his new in-laws, having married the daughter of a Mexican vice governor in 1831. However, in 1833, his young wife died during a cholera epidemic, and Bowie was never the same. His drinking and gambling increased, but nonetheless, he threw himself wholeheartedly behind the growing movement for Texas independence.

David Crockett was a one-off, true American original. He was eccentric, colorful, a genuine rough-and-tumble bear hunter, an Indian fighter, and a politician. Early nineteenth-century Americans gobbled up Almanacs and books describing his exaggerated frontier exploits making Davy Crockett a household name throughout the young country. In 1835, Crockett was pushing fifty years old and dead broke. He had just lost his bid for reelection to Congress, partly because he made the political mistake of

David Crockett
(Courtesy of Library of
Congress, LCUSZ62-
7368)

clashing with the popular President Andrew Jackson over his old commander's Indian Removal Bill, which Crockett viewed as unjust to the Indians.

Crockett told the Tennessee voters that "they might all go to Hell and I will go to Texas." And he did.

Despite their personality differences, one thing Bowie and Travis did agree on was that the defense of the Alamo was vital to the survival of Texas independence. Both perceived that the Alamo was all that stood between the advancing Santa Anna and General Sam Houston, the newly appointed commander of the Texas army, who was attempting, with varying degrees of effort, to organize an army, a hundred miles away at Washington on the Bravos.

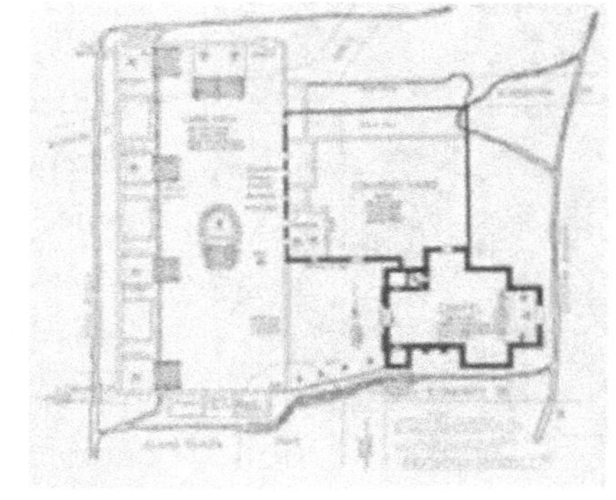

Alamo plot plan (Courtesy of University of North Texas Libraries)

Brass line in front of the Alamo Chapel memorializing Travis' line in the sand.

Travis and Bowie undertook the daunting task of transforming the nearly three-acre massive mission compound into a fortress. The complex was almost completely surrounded by limestone walls three to four feet thick and nine to twelve feet high. Along the south wall ran a one-story building named the Low Barracks, and along the east wall ran a two-story building, formerly used as a convent, called the Long Barracks. The sturdiest building was the Alamo Chapel, standing twenty-two feet high, with walls four feet thick. The formidable structure's days as a functioning church had long since passed; it was roofless, and the dirt floor was filled with debris. Originally, Bowie was ordered by Houston to destroy the Alamo, but Bowie decided that the Alamo was 'the key to Texas', and he would rather "die in these ditches than give it up to the enemy."

What the Texans did have was firepower, having accumulated over twenty cannons. What they didn't have were the bodies to properly man the cannons and adequately defend the sprawling Alamo complex. On February 24, Bowie succumbed to a 'disease of a peculiar nature', which is now thought to be tuberculosis, and spent the rest of the siege confined to his cot in an interior room of the Low Barracks, leaving the young Travis in sole command.

Legend holds that after twelve days of constant bombardment from Mexican cannons, on the eve of the final assault, Travis called his men together in the Alamo courtyard, unsheathed his sword, and dramatically drew a line in the sand. It appeared that despite his pleas for reinforcements, the defense of the Alamo rested solely with them. All those who wished to stay and fight, against an overwhelming force, pledged to give no quarter, were to cross the line. All crossed, but one. Louis 'Moses' Rose did not cross the line but rather went over the wall, somehow managing to elude the Mexicans sentries, and lived to tell the heroic tale of the line in the sand.

In the dim pre-dawn light of March 6, the Mexican army, fueled by the savage bugle call, signaling no quarter, of the 'deguello', stormed the fortress. Twice the gallant defenders repelled the attackers. On the third charge, however, the north wall was breached. Once the Mexicans were in the compound, the end was near. The Texians retreated into the Long Barracks, determined to make a last stand. Bloody hand-to-hand fighting ensued as the Mexicans swept through the Long Barracks room by room.

Colonel David Crockett's military experience had consisted of a brief stint as a scout and hunter for General Andrew Jackson during the Creek War over twenty years before. Nonetheless, Crockett and his 'Tennessee Boys' were assigned to defend the most perilous position in the compound: the stretch between the chapel and the gatehouse protected only by a low wooden palisade.

Dawn at the Alamo, by Henry Arthur McArdle (Library of Congress, LC-DIG-27909)

The Mexicans breached the north wall, scrambled into the plaza, and made a bloody sweep through the Long Barracks. Crockett and his Tennesseans attempted to get to the Long Barracks, but they never made it. Cut off from the Long Barracks, with their backs against the chapel walls, the gritty frontiersmen dug in for a last stand. When their ammunition ran out, the Tennessee Boys used their long rifles as clubs and finally knives and fists in their desperate but ultimately fatal struggle against their relentless attackers.

The advancing Mexicans then fell on the last of the defenders, who had retreated into the chapel, using the Texians' own cannons to blast their way past the barricaded wooden doors. The battle was over.

Susannah Dickinson, the fifteen-year-old wife of defender Captain Almeron Dickinson and her infant daughter had survived the carnage, along with other women and children by huddling together in one of the side rooms of the chapel.

Santa Anna, who did not actively participate in the siege, entered the Alamo Plaza, with his standard display of pomp and circumstance, and demanded to be shown the lifeless bodies of Travis, Bowie, and Crockett.

Travis was found, at his post, slumped over a cannon on the north wall, a single bullet hole in his forehead, apparently among the first to fall. His slave,

Joe, another fortunate survivor of the battle, would later recall that his master's last words were, "Come on, boys, the Mexicans are upon us, and we'll give them hell!"

Bowie's mutilated body was located on his cot, in an interior room of the Low Barracks. The legend holds that the great knife fighter fought desperately to the end, with his signature weapon and a pair of pistols given to him by none other than the Honorable David Crockett. As with many of the Alamo legends, the particulars of Bowie's demise, and the intensity of his final struggle, in light of his compromised health, are still debated by Alamo aficionados and historians. Bowie's mother, however, had no doubts concerning her son's conduct during his final moments. When the seventy-year-old widow was informed of her son's death, she coolly remarked, "I'll wager they found no wounds in his back."

Crockett's body was located, by most accounts, in front of the chapel, the site of the Tennesseans' ferocious last stand. According to Travis' slave Joe, "Crockett and a few of his friends were found together with twenty-four of the enemy dead around them." Mrs. Dickinson would also recall that she saw Crockett's bloodied corpse, by the chapel, with 'his peculiar hat' at his side.

The final casualties for the Mexicans were probably around six hundred and, for the gallant Texians, somewhere around two hundred. Once again, historians continue to argue the exact statistics. The basic problem is that Santa Anna's battle reports exaggerated the Texans' body count and downplayed his own fatalities. The official casualty toll for the Texans has been listed as hundred and eighty-nine since 1936. The list was compiled through military, court, and land records, and family correspondence. Ongoing research indicates that the actual count could be as high as two hundred and fifty but also reveals that some names should be removed from the sacred list of Texas martyrs. Nobody in Texas wants to tackle that thorny issue.

Thus, the official list of the heroes of the Battle of the Alamo remains the same.

Despite his disproportionate casualties and clearly underestimating the toll the hard-fought battle had on his army's morale, Santa Anna surmised that the Alamo was 'a small affair'. Six weeks later, amid Texians' cries of 'Remember the Alamo', Santa Anna was routed in the somewhat bizarre eighteen-minute battle of San Jacinto. The self-proclaimed 'Napoleon of the West' and his army were caught taking a siesta at three-thirty in the afternoon, and the Texas War for Independence was won.

WHAT HAPPENED NEXT?

Almost as soon as the smoke cleared from the funeral pyres, the fallen defenders of the Alamo were considered as martyrs to liberty. The Alamo was perceived as much more than a ninety-minute battle in the fight for Texas independence. It symbolized freedom versus tyranny but also bought precious time for Sam Houston to organize his army. The historical impact of the siege of the Alamo on the future of the United States cannot be overstated.

In 1845, Texas became the twenty-eighth state of the United States sparking a war with Mexico, resulting in the Union obtaining the future Western States of New Mexico, Arizona, Utah, Nevada, and California. The fallen Texians of the Alamo were sacrificed for the cause of America's fulfillment of its Manifest Destiny. The spirit of the Alamo was remembered; the physical Alamo was forgotten (almost).

In May 1836, the defeated Mexican army destroyed much of what remained of the Alamo buildings. Still standing were the ruins of the chapel, the battered walls, and most of the Long Barracks. Over the next decade, the locals pilfered the remains of the Alamo for building supplies until the US army took possession of the complex for use as a headquarters and supply depot. The army remained for almost three decades and, despite toying with the initial idea of destroying all the buildings, made many improvements, including the installation of a roof on the chapel and adding the now universally recognized 'hump' atop the chapel's front parapet to conceal the visually unattractive peak of the roof.

The army vacated the Alamo in 1879, and the Catholic Church sold the Long Barracks to a San Antonio businessman, who turned what was left of the historic ruins into a two-story shopping center. He also rented the chapel, the centerpiece of the iconic battle, and turned it into a grocery warehouse. Yes, you read that correctly, the 'Shrine of Texas Liberty' was, essentially, a nineteenth-century Walmart.

1901 photograph by Ernst Wilhelm, showing a portion of the Hugo Schmelzer building

Finally, some sanity started to emerge among the citizenry of San Antonio and pressure was put on the city and the State of Texas by private groups, particularly the Daughters of the Republic of Texas (DRT), to reclaim and preserve the Alamo. Through the considerable efforts of the DRT, by 1905, the church and what was left of the compound, including the Long Barracks, was owned by the State of Texas, and custody of the entire property was given to the DRT 'to be maintained in good order and repair, without charge to the State'. The saga of the preservation of the Alamo did not end there, however.

Despite the success of the DRT in its preservation efforts, the leadership was in turmoil. DRT was split into two different factions, each with different passionate visions concerning the manner in which the Alamo should be remembered. Specifically, one group, led by Adina de Zavala, sought to preserve all surviving structures of the Alamo compound, especially the Long Barracks, and the other, led by Clara Driscoll, wanted to preserve only the chapel and actually tear down what was left of the Long Barracks. Both women were right, and both women were wrong, each interpreting the battle and the physical layout of the Alamo compound at the time of the siege to suit their own goals.

Clara Driscoll ultimately won what San Antonio wags had named 'the second battle of the Alamo'; the Long Barracks were torn down, and today, she is fondly remembered as the 'Savior of the Alamo'. The chapel has become the universally recognized symbol of the thirteen-day battle of the Alamo. The saga of the preservation of the Alamo was still not over, however.

After over a century of being the caretakers of Texas' most cherished historical site, the Daughters of the Republic of Texas were, basically, kicked out of the Alamo in 2015. In a series of investigations by the State of Texas, the State charged the DRT with financial mismanagement and maintenance malfeasance. Consequently, the Texas General Land Office (GLO) took over the custodianship of the Alamo in 2011.

A half billion dollar project is underway to restore the Alamo compound to its 1836 three-acre footprint, which entails closing off traffic on Alamo Street and removing or relocating the structures and businesses that occupy the 1836 location of the West Wall. Not surprisingly, the ambitious project, scheduled to be completed in 2026, has its share of critics. Stay tuned.

WHAT DO I DO WHEN I GET THERE?

The Alamo, 300 Alamo Plaza, San Antonio, TX 78205 (thealamo.org)

Thanks to Clara Driscoll, the chapel, 'hump' and all, is the focal point of the Alamo, around which, over the last century and a half, the sleepy town of San Antonio de Bexar evolved into a bustling cow town and finally into a modern city, with almost one and half million residents. Tourists enter the chapel through two large wooden doors, gently reminded by a brass sign that the chapel is a shrine dedicated to those that gave their life inside its walls, gentlemen are to remove their hats and silence is urged. Admission is free, and audio headsets, which guide visitors through the Alamo grounds, are available for purchase. Enthusiastic and knowledgeable docents are stationed throughout, available to answer any questions.

Inside the chapel, the cool thick limestone walls are lined with oil paintings of Alamo defenders. Although some visitors are initially disappointed with the physically diminutive size of the chapel, there exists a palatable sense of reverence and awe inside the only remaining structure of that horrific battle.

When you exit the back door of the chapel, you enter a small courtyard that has displays describing the history of the mission and authentic cannons scattered about. The reconstructed Long Barracks now serves as a museum, dedicated to the history of Texas, particularly the Texas Revolution.

Of course, there is the obligatory gift shop on the grounds, where you purchase anything from Alamo placemats to expensive sculptures. Perhaps you're in the market for a coonskin cap? The shop does house, however, a highly detailed six-foot by four-foot diorama depicting the 1836 siege.

Situated in Alamo Plaza, directly in front of the Alamo, is the sixty-foot-high marble and granite cenotaph, commemorating the battle. Erected in 1936, the Alamo Cenotaph bears the names of the perished martyrs and carvings of its most famous defenders. In 1982, the cenotaph was the scene of an unfortunate incident when the highly medicated heavy metalist Ozzy Osbourne was arrested for urinating on the memorial, resulting in his being banned from San Antonio for a decade. Don't mess with Texas!

The Cenotaph

IS THERE ANYTHING ELSE?

Outside the Alamo, since you are literally in downtown San Antonio, there is no shortage of stores and other attractions within eyesight of the Alamo. In fact, the lineup of stores along what was the west wall continues to infuriate the proponents of the renovation of Alamo Plaza (especially Ripley's Believe It or Not). However, no Alamo-themed visit to San Antonio would be complete, without a visit to the following:

IMAX: Alamo: The Price of Freedom, Shops at Rivercenter, 849 Commerce St., San Antonio, TX 78205 (amctheatres.com)

There are some Alamo-themed spots that you simply can't miss. At the Rivercenter Mall, a couple of blocks from the Alamo, you can see an IMAX presentation, 'Alamo: The Price of Freedom', on an immense screen, ten times the size of a normal screen. The forty-eight-minute film is well done, historically accurate, and a good place to start your Alamo visit if you have the willpower not to go straight to the Alamo.

Briscoe Western Art Museum, 210 W. Market St., San Antonio, TX 78205 (briscoemuseum.org)

Briscoe Western Art Museum

Housed in the beautifully restored old library building, the museum showcases Western paintings, photography, and sculptures. A pleasant surprise is a room dedicated to the Alamo, which includes an authentic cannon from the battle and a diorama.

San Fernando Cathedral, 115 W. Main Plaza, San Antonio, TX 78205 (sfcathedral.org)

The Defenders' Ashes

A pleasant mile walk west from the Alamo is the San Fernando Cathedral, the oldest church in Texas, and from whose tower Santa Anna's red flag of no quarter once flew. The original steeple was torn down during renovations in the mid-nineteenth century, but the old church still holds some allure for Alamo enthusiasts, including that Jim Bowie was married there in 1831. Mystery has always surrounded the question of what happened to the Defender's ashes. About a year after the battle, the ashes were collected and buried in unknown locations.

One version of the fate of the ashes came from Texas leader Juan Sequin, who decades later said that he entombed the ashes and buried them at San Fernando Cathedral. In 1936, during renovations at the church, remains were discovered. The remains were placed in a fancy marble sarcophagus, which is on display in the left vestibule, just inside the front door.

WHERE CAN I WET MY WHISTLE?

There is no shortage of drinking establishments in San Antonio, Western-themed or not. The world-renowned San Antonio River Walk, a couple of blocks from the Alamo, is a network of walkways along the banks of San

Antonio, one story below street level, that are lined with shops, restaurants, and bars. It is an unavoidable tourist stop if you are in San Antonio, but if $22 margaritas are not your speed, the following authentic Western saloons are highly recommended.

The Menger Bar, 204 Alamo Plaza, San Antonio, TX 78205 (mengerhotel.com)

Sitting in the shadow of the Alamo, the Menger Bar is the oldest continuously operated saloon in San Antonio. It opened in 1858 as part of the luxurious Menger Hotel and was such a popular watering hole for Texas cattlemen that the bar witnessed more cattle deals than any other location in the United States. The old heavily varnished mahogany bar looks like it belongs on a Western movie set although it was remodeled in the 1880s to replicate a British pub.

The list of past patrons who have hoisted a few in this cozy wood-paneled oasis is a 'Who's Who' of American history: Ulysses S. Grant, Robert E. Lee, Sam Houston, Jesse and Frank James, Babe Ruth, and even John Wayne! Teddy Roosevelt recruited many of his Rough Riders at the bar and was reprimanded for buying his men too much beer. (Is there such a thing?) If you can pry yourself away from the bullet-scarred bar, take a walk through the lobby of the still magnificent Menger Hotel lobby and peruse the great old photographs of the hotel's famous past guests and the display of Rough Rider memorabilia.

The Buckhorn Saloon & Museum, 318 E. Houston St., San Antonio, TX 78205 (buckhornmuseum.com)

If you have an unnatural fear of antlers, skip this joint. Otherwise, go and soak in the authentic Old West atmosphere of this huge saloon that also houses the world's largest collection of horns and antlers. The legend is that when the bar opened in 1881, the bartender would accept antlers as payment from cash-strapped thirsty cowpokes. As if the collection of horns, antlers, and stuffed animals weren't enough to hold your interest while you're sipping on a Lone Star, the saloon also encompasses the Texas Ranger Museum, where for a modest fee you can gaze upon hundreds of guns, badges, and other artifacts associated with the Texas Rangers.

The Buckhorn Saloon

WHAT ABOUT GRUB?

Once again, San Antonio, particularly the River Walk, has more than enough eating establishments to fit any taste or budget. Zeroing in on a couple of restaurants, you might otherwise miss. You should give these a try.

Mi Tierra Cafe and Bakery, 218 Produce Row, San Antonio, TX 78207 (mitierracafe.com)

Located in the festive Market Square, Mia Tierra is a huge twenty-four-hour bar, bakery and restaurant, dishing out generous portions of authentic Mexican cuisine. It is a bit touristy, but the food is good and the atmosphere is fun. Give it a whirl and don't forget to tip the Mariachi band.

Schilo's Delicatessen, 424 E. Commerce St., San Antonio, TX 78205 (schilos.com)

Located downtown, in an old historic building, this landmark deli has been serving delicious German fare for over hundred years. Originally catering to

San Antonio's German population, the reasonably priced deli, still packs them in. A Rueben sandwich and a homemade root beer will set you back about ten bucks. Try that on the Riverwalk!

WHERE CAN I HANG MY HAT AND PUT MY BOOTS UNDER A BED?

With over twenty-four million visitors a year, there is no shortage of hotel rooms available, within walking distance to the Alamo. Some suggestions:

Menger Hotel, 204 Alamo Plaza, San Antonio, TX 78205, (210)223-4361 (mengerhotel.com)

Yes, there is a hotel attached to the wonderful bar. It is an old hotel, so the rooms are somewhat dated, compared to a modern chain hotel, but the ambiance and the sense of history of the place more than make up for it. And there is the bar.

The Menger Hotel

Two hotels that are close to the Alamo and Riverwalk (without Riverwalk prices) and serve free breakfast are as follows.

- Springfield Suites, 411 Bowie Street, San Antonio, Texas, (210)2222121 (marriott.com)
- Fairfield Inn and Suites by Marriott, 422 Bonham St., San Antonio, TX 78205, (210)212-6262 (marriott.com)

WHAT SHOULD I WATCH AND READ BEFORE I HIT THE TRAIL?

BOOKS

- *A Time to Stand: The Epic of the Alamo* (1961, by Walter Lord)—Lord unabashedly embraces Alamo legends that some modern historians have placed in doubt, but it is an easy read and a good starting point to get the basics of the battle. Many of those skeptical modern historians first got hooked on the Alamo thanks to Lord's compelling telling of the siege and his vivid portrayal of its main heroes: Crockett, Bowie, and Travis.

- *Three Roads to the Alamo: The Lives and Fortunes of David Crockett, James Bowie, and William Barret Travis* (1998, by William C. Davis)—it provides a more in-depth examination of the 1836 siege, but the focus is the how and why the Alamo's three most famous ended up among the noble defenders.

- *Eyewitness to the Alamo* (2001, by Bill Groneman)—*Groneman* is a retired New York firefighter and Alamo aficionado who has written sever*al books* abou*t the Alamo and* David Crockett *(Death of a Legend: The Myth and Mystery Surrounding the Death of Davy Crockett,* and *David Crockett: Hero of the Common Man)*. This book offers over hundred recorded eyewitness accounts of the battle.

VIDEOS

- *The Alamo* (1960)—the granddaddy of them all; John Wayne's epic salute to the Alamo defenders. The Duke produced, directed, and starred as Davy Crockett in this monumental film. Historically, it's a mess, but it clearly captures the fighting spirit of the gallant martyrs for freedom.

- *Davy Crockett: King of the Wild Frontier* (1954–1955)—when this three-part Walt Disney series aired, it sparked a marketing phenomenon the likes of which had never been seen. The last episode featured the Alamo, and the closing scene of Fess Parker, as Davy Crockett, swinging Old Betsy at the oncoming Mexican soldiers, as the pictures fade, is burned into the memory of many a baby boomer. It's worth another look.

- *The Alamo* (2004)—it is not a remake of Wayne's classic; it's not sugarcoated. Instead, it portrays the main defenders as sometimes flawed individuals who have found themselves in heroic circumstances, particularly Billy Bob Thornton's portrayal of a self-doubting Crockett. However, the climactic battle scene, shot in darkness, is worth the price of the rental.

TIPS FROM THE TRAIL

The Alamo is a 'must-see' for any Old West enthusiast and San Antonio is a fun town. Hard-core Alamo buffs may be disappointed in the present carnival-like atmosphere surrounding the chapel. However, not without controversy, Alamo Plaza is currently undergoing sweeping changes in an effort to make the visiting experience more respectful. In the meantime, a trip inside the venerable and historic Alamo Chapel is a religious-like experience for those who grew up on Disney's 'Davy Crockett' and John Wayne movies. The two weeks leading up to March 6 is a time of frenzied activity at the Alamo with special programs and specialized tours culminating with a dawn ceremony on March 6.

THE DEATH OF DAVID CROCKETT

The Fall of the Alamo, 1903, by Robert Jenkins Onderonk

By far, the most famous casualty of the Alamo siege was Colonel David Crockett. The grisly details surrounding Crockett's demise have always been a source of controversy. Some contemporaries simply refused to believe that the seemingly indestructible frontiersman could have perished. Newspapers, for years afterward, would publish accounts of supposed Crockett sightings, including a report that Crockett was a Mexican prisoner working in a mine!

There still is significant and somewhat impassioned controversy concerning the details of Crockett's death. Specifically, the historical debate is whether Crockett actually surrendered, rather than heroically fighting to the bitter and inevitable end. It is now generally accepted by Alamo scholars that at the end of the siege, about seven Texan combatants were captured and brought before Santa Anna, who promptly and unceremoniously ordered their execution. In 1975, an English translation of a Mexican officer's 'diary' was published, which immediately sparked significant controversy among Alamo scholars. The translated Jose de la Pena diary added a new wrinkle: "the naturalist David Crockett, well known in North America for his unusual adventures… " was among the seven. The unspoken but nonetheless glaring implication is that the surrender of the Alamo's most famous defender taints the cherished, almost mystical image of a heroic last stand to the death.

Critics of the de la Pena 'diary' are quick to point out that there are severe problems with the authenticity of the 'diary'. In particular, the original documents were not authored contemporaneously with the events and were not even written entirely in de Pena's handwriting. Some historians who have embraced the de la Pena diary have accused those who refuse to accept the authenticity of the diary as unable to get over their childhood image of Walt Disney's 'Davy Crockett'. In turn, the diary proponents have been labeled as revisionists intent on tarnishing one of America's most cherished legends.

In any event, it is indisputable that David Crockett perished while fighting against overwhelming odds for freedom at the Alamo on March 6, 1836. Crockett's body was unceremoniously assembled with the other Texan bodies and burned in two funeral pyres, the ashes left to scatter in the brisk Texas wind. Here is a helpful hint, though: don't ask one of the docents at the Alamo if Davy Crockett surrendered.

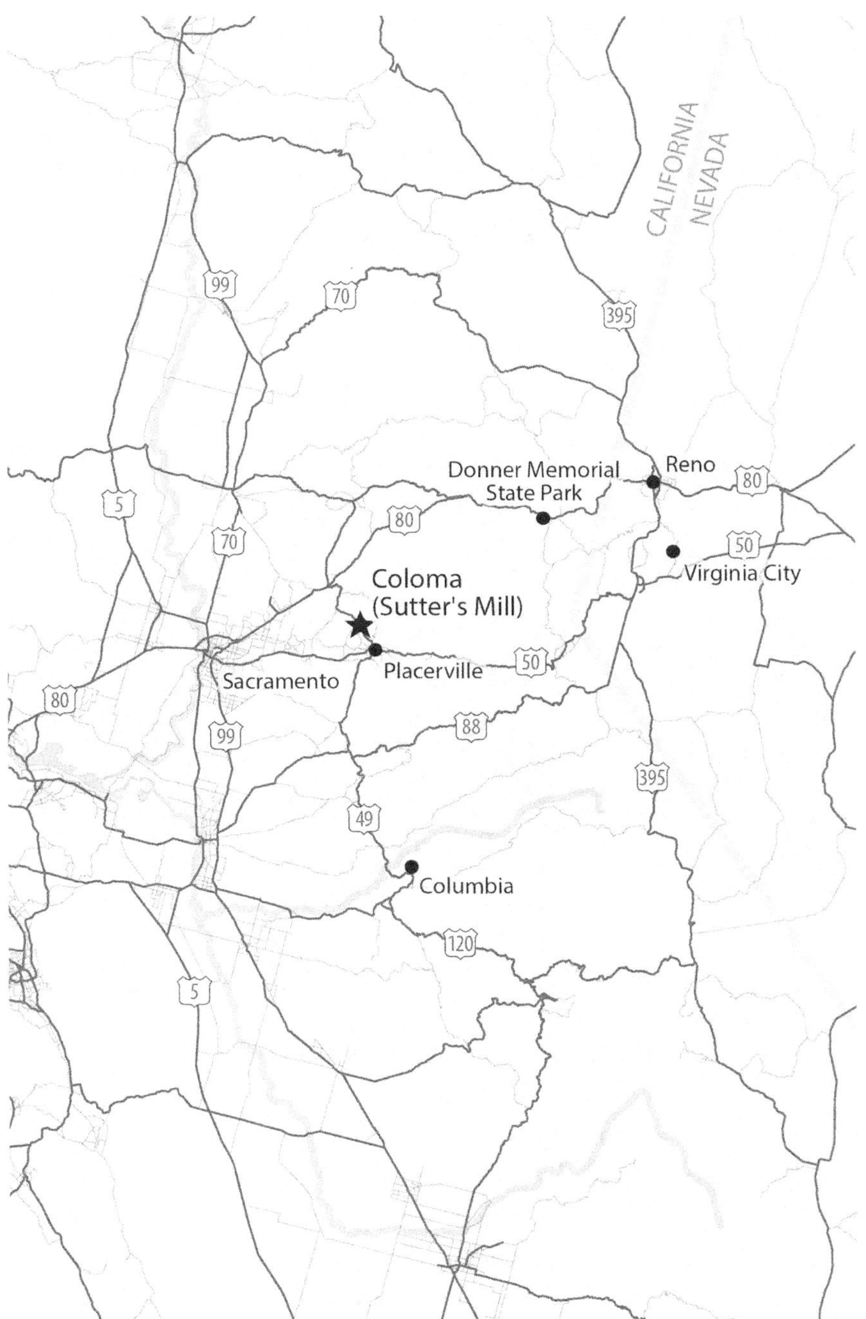

CALIFORNIA
NEVADA
99
70
395
5
70
80
Donner Memorial
State Park
Reno
80
50
Coloma
(Sutter's Mill)
Virginia City
Sacramento
Placerville
50
99
88
80
395
49
Columbia
5
120

Marshall Park Gold Discovery State Historic Park

Gold miners, El Dorado, California (Library of Congress)

WHAT HAPPENED HERE?

On the cold morning of January 24, 1848, in Coloma, California, James W. Marshall, while inspecting a mill he was constructing on the south fork of the American River, spotted shiny golden specs in the tailrace. He quickly scooped them up and placed them in the crown of his hat. He would later recall, "It made my heart thump, for I was certain it was gold." It was. The great California gold rush was on.

Marshall, a carpenter by trade, was business partners with John Augustus Sutter, who, in 1848, was already a wealthy man. The forty-five-year-old

Swiss immigrant reigned supreme over a fifty-thousand-acre kingdom in California's Sacramento Valley.

John Augustus Sutter, c. 1859 (Library of Congress, LC-USZ262-13333639)

Sutter had arrived in Mexican-controlled California in 1839 and promptly made powerful connections with governmental authorities, including the California governor, who awarded Sutter a huge tract of land on what was then the northern frontier of the Mexican province. It is hard to imagine today that California was considered the middle of nowhere fewer than two hundred years ago. It was Mexico's northernmost province, three thousand miles from the eastern seaboard, most of it unchartered terrain. Because Mexico had just lost Texas to the United States, California's governor surmised (albeit incorrectly) that the building of a trading establishment in Northern California would forestall any American encroachment into the territory.

Specifically, Sutter was authorized to "function as authority and dispenser of justice, in order to prevent the robberies committed by adventurers from the United States, to stop the invasion of savage Indians and the hunting and trapping by companies from the Columbia." Sutter took his role quite seriously. He demanded he be addressed as 'Captain', and he commanded a private army of over two hundred Indians, supervised by German-speaking white officers, tasked with defending his compound, which he built at the confluence of two rivers: the American (ironically) and the Sacramento, near present-day Sacramento, about fifty miles from the sleepy harbor town of Yerba Buena (now San Francisco). Sutter christened the site New Helvetia (Spanish for 'New Switzerland').

Using laborers he had brought with him, as well as local Indians, Sutter constructed an impressive headquarters: a fort with adobe walls two-feet thick and eighteen-foot high enclosing adobe homes and offices, a gunsmith, a distillery, blacksmith and carpenters' shops, and a tannery. Outside the walls were over twelve thousand head of cattle, two thousand horses and mules, ten thousand sheep, a thousand hogs, and hundreds of acres of fertile wheat fields.

At its peak, during the wheat harvest, Sutter would employ as many as six hundred Indians to tend the crop.

Sutter had entered into a partnership with Marshall to produce lumber for his expanding empire. Marshall selected a location in the Coloma Valley, on the banks of the American River, about forty-five miles east of Sutter's Fort, to construct a sawmill, which operated by utilizing the river to power the wheel and drive the saw.

Sutter's Fort, c. 1847 (Library of Congress, LC-USZ262-1133)

The tailrace diverted water back to the river. That fateful morning, while inspecting the mill, Marshall noticed something sparkly in about six inches of icy water in the bed of the tailrace. He picked out two small pieces that sparkled golden in the sunlight and examined them closely. He beat the golden pieces with a rock, but the pieces flattened rather than broke or crumbled. He went up to his workers and announced, "I have found it."

"What is 'it'?" his workers replied.

Marshall's response: "Gold." He was sure of it.

One worker took a flake back to his cabin, where his wife was making soap. She threw it in a boiling pot of lye, and the flake emerged as golden as ever. In his diary, a worker named Henry Bigler noted for posterity the spectacular find: 'on Monday 24th, some kind of metal was found in the tail race that looks like gold first discovered by James Martial, the boss of the mill.'

James Marshall at Sutter's Mill, c 1850 (Denver Public Library)

Four days later, Marshall showed up at Sutter's Fort to confer with his partner. The two men curiously examined the gold flakes and consulted an encyclopedia to ascertain the qualities of gold. They doused the golden flakes with nitric acid, but the flakes remained unchanged. To determine how dense the gold metal was, the pair placed it on one tray of an apothecary scale and balanced the other side with silver coins. They then submerged the scale in water. The tray with the gold metal sank, establishing it was denser than the silver. Sutter was now convinced his find was, indeed, pure gold.

Sutter swore his men to secrecy to buy time to figure out the best way to handle the astounding discovery. But it didn't remain a secret for long, especially after the mill workers started panning for gold in their off time and using their finds to pay for provisions. The amazing news hit San Francisco first, and its few hundred residents promptly headed to Sutter's Mill. The residents of Los Angeles and Monterey quickly followed suit, and soon, there were thousands scouring for gold. Because San Francisco was a port city, the news next spread to those places accessible to California by ship: Hawaii, Oregon, Mexico, Chile, Peru,

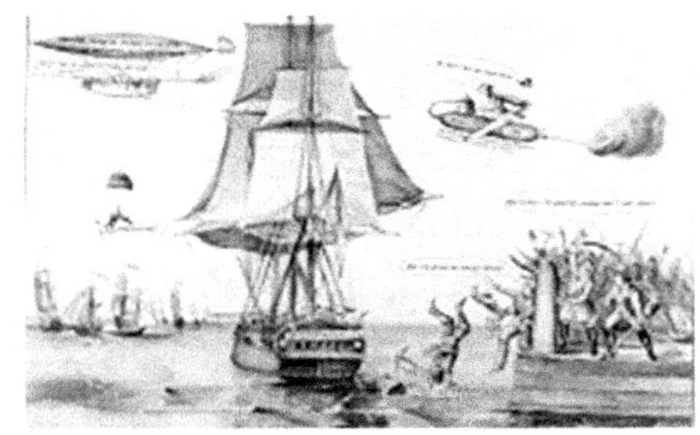

The Way They Go to California, 1849 (Library of Congress, LCUSZ62-8972)

Australia, New Zealand, and China. The news was slower to reach the populous East Coast, where the revelation was met with skepticism until President James K. Polk confirmed the discovery in his State of the Union address.

By the beginning of 1849, gold fever had infected the Atlantic Seaboard through the South and the Mississippi Valley. The immediate concern was how to get to California. The quickest way to traverse the West Coast was by ship. The most popular route was around the southern tip of South America, then north over the Pacific to California, some thirteen thousand miles, a trip that could take four to eight months depending on weather conditions and the type of ship. Others chose a quicker but more expensive and perilous route across Mexico or the Isthmus of Panama that shaved months off the journey.

Still, others simply hitched their wagons and headed west. But come they did. In the month of February 1849 alone, more than fifty ships of all types sailed from New York, bound for the promised land.

By the end of 1849, the non-native population of California had grown from about seven thousand five hundred to over a hundred thousand. It is estimated that over three hundred thousand gold seekers, dubbed, 'forty-niners' ultimately found their way to the gold fields. By 1852, San Francisco had become a rowdy, vibrant city with close to forty thousand residents. It would soon have more millionaires than Boston or New York.

The gold rush would be the largest migration in US history, drawing fortune seekers from a dozen countries—in 1852 alone, twenty thousand Chinese immigrants passed through the San Francisco customs house—contributing to a multiethnic society on America's West Coast. Eventually, there would be a backlash against the foreign immigrants, and the passage of a Foreign Miners Tax imposed a steep levy on all 'non-Americans'. The Native American population would also take a devastating hit from which it would never recover. It has been estimated that over a hundred twenty thousand would perish of disease, starvation, and homicide during the gold rush years.

Once they arrived at the goldfields, the Argonauts made do with a shovel and a wash pan. The gold dust and nuggets they retrieved in their pans were placer gold that is remnants of a mineral vein in the Sierra Nevada that had been carried downward over the eons and deposited in layers of creek sediment. It was slow, backbreaking work. A panful of gold could fetch the miner about a thousand dollars although a day's work usually earned him about fifteen. Through the years, as the surface gold became more difficult to find, more elaborate equipment was required to dig deeper.

1854 Daguerreotype Showing the Use of High-Pressure Water (Canadian Photo Gallery Institute)

By 1857, large mining companies had taken over the process, ultimately employing hydraulic techniques, which had a devastating effect on the ecosystem, prompting flooding, the ruination of crops, and the permanent scarring of the once beautiful landscape. An incredible amount of gold was pulled from the ground between 1849 and 1852, with an estimated worth of over two hundred million dollars. By the outbreak of the Civil War in 1861, California's mines had produced in excess of six hundred million dollars' worth of precious metal.

It is an uncontested historical fact that merchants made much more money than miners during the gold rush. Clever businessmen quickly purchased prospecting supplies in San Francisco and resold them at an enormous profit in newly established retail stores in Coloma and Sacramento (see p. 74). Other entrepreneurs, anxious to separate miners from their gold dust, soon offered shipping services, entertainment, lodging, food preparation, and, of course, saloons, gambling houses, and brothels. You might recognize the name of the San Francisco merchant who, in 1853, started selling durable denim overalls to miners: Levi Strauss.

Coincidentally, a week after Marshall's discovery, the Treaty of Guadalupe Hidalgo was signed, ending the Mexican-American War and awarding the backwater agricultural province of California to the United States. The United States, and not snake-bit Mexico, would be the beneficiary of the hundreds of millions of dollars of gold extracted from California over the next decade. Although good news for the expanding country, the transfer of California from Mexico caused complications for Sutter and Marshall since the legal status of his Mexican land grants was in limbo, and there was no legal authority in place to oversee land claims. The partners tried, in vain, to assert their ownership rights, but they were ill-prepared for the onslaught of fortune seekers that were about to descend upon the American River. They never made a penny on the discovery.

Not long after Marshall's discovery, all of Sutter's employees abandoned him to seek their fortunes in the goldfields. Squatters roamed his property, destroying his crops and slaughtering his livestock. By 1852, these interlopers had destroyed New Helvetia, and Sutter was left bankrupt. He would later lament, "There is a saying that men will steal everything but a milestone and a millstone; they stole my millstones."

The once-powerful Sutter spent the rest of his life, with varying degrees of success, attempting to enforce his land grants and seeking compensation for his role in colonizing California. In 1864, the California legislature voted to award him the paltry sum of fifteen thousand dollars, payable over five years. It wasn't until 1880 that a US Congressional committee introduced a bill that would pay Sutter fifty thousand dollars and, at long last, give the man who was referred to as the father of California his due. However, as Sutter's luck would have it, the old captain died of natural causes before the bill was passed at the age of seventy-seven.

Marshall was similarly unsuccessful in trying to claim ownership of the land around Sutter's Mill. The sawmill itself was cut down; the lumber was used to build cabins. After about a year, he gave up trying to keep the flood of prospectors off what he believed to be his land and started panning for gold like everybody else. He did so unsuccessfully. In the ensuing years, he took on different jobs, including blacksmithing, but by 1872, he was dead broke and drinking heavily (a common frontier theme). So serious was his desperation that he had stooped to sell his autograph for a dollar.

That same year, the California legislature approved for Marshall a two-hundred-dollar-a-month pension, 'in recognition of his considerable service to the state'. Marshall blew it, however, when, in 1882, he showed up belligerently drunk to the assembly chamber to complain about the planned discontinuance of the stipend. He died, penniless, in 1885 at the age of seventy-four. He was buried near the site of his momentous discovery.

However, James W. Marshall was not completely forgotten by his fellow Californians. In 1890, through the efforts of the Native Sons of the Golden West, a ten-foot statue of Marshall holding a nugget in one hand and pointing with the other to the gold discovery site was erected over the final resting place of the man who started it all.

James W. Marshall c. 1880
(Sacramento Public Library)

WHAT HAPPENED NEXT?

James W. Marshall Monument, Coloma California

The impact of Marshall's find on the future of California, and the entire United States, cannot be overemphasized. The resulting gold rush is considered by many historians to be the most significant event of the first half of the nineteenth century. It, almost overnight, drew hundreds of thousands of people to California, forever changing the demographics of America's West. Fueled by the sudden population and economic boom, within three years, California bypassed the territorial stage and was admitted under the Compromise of 1850 as the nation's thirty-first state.

The Compromise of 1850 was actually a complicated set of five different laws that allowed California to join the Union as a free state, upsetting the tenuous sectional balance between slave and free factions. The fast-track admission of California into the Union as a free state propelled the United States even closer to the inevitable Civil War. In that struggle, California's rich gold deposits helped fund the Union war effort to such an extent that General U.S. Grant commented, "I do not know what we would do in this great national emergency if it were not for the gold sent from California."

California would also play more than just a geographical role in the expansion of the West. A group of Sacramento businessmen was the driving force behind the building of the transcontinental railroad, which when completed in 1869 connected California to the East Coast and spurred an economic boom that would make the United States the richest economy on the planet. The gold rush inspired the California Dream of instant wealth in a New World, the very sentiment that would eventually become the American Dream itself. That dream is still alive today with California continuing its place on the frontier of wealth and innovation. Historians have had to look no further than Silicon Valley to draw parallels between yesterday's forty-niners and today's tech entrepreneurs. As wonderfully penned by historian H.W. Brands:

The old American Dream… was the dream
Of Puritans, of Benjamin Franklin's 'Poor
Richard'… of men and women content
To accumulate their modest fortunes
a little at a time, year by year by year.
The new dream was the dream of instant wealth,
Won in a twinkling by audacity and good luck
[This] golden dream… became a prominent
part of the American psyche only after Sutter's Mill.

WHAT DO I DO WHEN I GET THERE?

Marshall Gold Site Museum

Marshall Gold Discovery State Historic Park, Hwy. 49/Coloma Road at Bridge Street, Coloma, CA 95613, (530)622-3470

The California State Park encompasses most of the historic town of Coloma and is the site of Sutter's sawmill, where Marshall first made his discovery.

Replica Sutter's Sawmill

I was actually pleasantly surprised at how nice it was, and I ended up spending more time there than I thought I would. Although once a site of almost unimaginable bustle and turmoil, the area now is serene, with several hiking trails that loop you through different areas of the park, past a number of historic buildings, including Marshall's cabin, an impressive monument, and a working blacksmith shop. Gold panning activities also take place year-round.

The showpiece of the park is the reconstructed sawmill, which is located about a hundred yards from its original site. After 1850, Sutter's Mill was no longer in service, and its wood was utilized for cabins and fuel. Over time, the American River changed course, and the mill's location was lost to history until, in 1924, the water level dropped, allowing for an archaeological dig that revealed the true location. A stone monument now marks the spot where Sutter's Mill once stood.

On the grounds of the park is the Gold Discovery Museum, a small but wonderful museum. The exhibits and original artifacts not only tell the story of Marshall's discovery but also examine the culture of the Indians that were native to the area. Among the museum's treasures are some of Marshall's personal tools and household items, an authentic nineteenth-century stagecoach, and original timbers that were salvaged from the mill.

Take your time walking through the park, wander down to the American River, and try your luck panning for gold.

When the Argonauts arrived, they quickly realized the surface gold that ran down from the Sierra Nevada wasn't confined to just the American

Stone Monument

River. Branches of the river and wilderness streams were also rich with placer gold. If a hit was made, a mining town would pop up almost overnight, and just as quickly turn into a ghost town when the well ran dry. Some towns survived, however, and are worth visiting.

If you are game for a gold rush road trip, you can take California Highway 49, dubbed the Golden Chain Highway, which runs for approximately three hundred miles from Vinton in the North to Oakhurst in the south (highway49.org).

In addition to Coloma, worthwhile stops include the following.

PLACERVILLE, CALIFORNIA:

Hangman's Tree
Placerville

The 1848 mining town is just eight miles from the gold discovery site. Originally christened Dry Diggin's, it was also known as 'Hangtown', a nod to the town's propensity for frontier justice.

The site of the 'hanging tree' is now occupied by the Hangman's Tree Ice Cream Saloon, complete with mannequins hanging from the second-story windows. The structure was an authentic saloon for a hundred years before the building was renovated in 2017. Oh, well. At least the ice cream is good. Main Street of this town is lined with boutiques and shops located in historic buildings with ties to the gold rush era. It's a touristy, friendly town, with free parking for your first two hours (although I still managed to get a parking ticket). In addition to admiring the nineteenth-century structures on Main Street, visitors can tour the 1888 Gold Bug Mine, which is on the outskirts of town, at 2635 Gold Bug Lane, Placerville.

Columbia State Historic Park (visitColumbiaCalifornia.com)

A well-preserved gold rush town, with loads of nineteenth-century shops and boutiques, staffed by merchants in 1850s attire.

ANGELS CAMP, CALIFORNIA:

This restored mining town is where a young Mark Twain got his inspiration for *The Celebrated Jumping Frog of Calaveras County*. It is also home to Angels Camp Museum and Carriage House (775 South Main St.), which is located on the site of the original Angel's Quartz Mine and exhibits artifacts associated with Northern California's mining history.

SACRAMENTO, CALIFORNIA:

Only about an hour southwest of Coloma, on Highway 50, Sacramento, emerged from New Helvetia, and has an impressive Western Place pedigree of its own. It was the last stop on what would be the ill-fated Pony Express, and it was the starting point for the Southern Pacific Railroad's ambitious and successful venture to connect the country by rail. Sacramento has preserved its Western heritage in 'Old Sacramento', a well-preserved section of the capital city. Within about eight square blocks, Old Sacramento has some authentic old buildings and first-class museums.

Sutter's Fort State Historic Park, 28th Street, Sacramento, California (916)445-4422

Sutter's Fort was reconstructed in the 1890s and is operated by the California Parks and Recreation Department. A self-guided audio tour is available.

Sacramento History Museum, 101 I Street, Sacramento, California, (916)808-7059

Housed in a restoration of the 1857 Sacramento Building, the museum displays Sacramento's compelling history through artifacts and hands-on exhibits.

California Railroad Museum, Old Sacramento

California State Railroad Museum, 125 I Street, Sacramento, California (916)323-9280

Very proud of its vital connection to the building of the Continental Railroad, the museum displays both refurbished and replicated engines and plush passenger coaches from the nineteenth century.

Wells Fargo Museum, 1000 2nd Street, Sacramento, California, (916)440-4263

The small, free museum features a display chronicling the impressive Western history of the bank and security service.

Donner Memorial State Park, 12593 Donner Pass Road, Truckee, California

About an hour and a half west of Coloma sits Donner Memorial State Park, located on the site of the ill-fated Donner Party's winter 1846 camp. Led by George Donner, a mixed bag of emigrants formed a wagon train from the Midwest to California. Along the way, they diverted from the usual route, taking what they thought was a shortcut. It wasn't. It added a full three weeks to their journey, causing them to reach the Sierra Nevada Mountain Range in Truckee Meadows in late October when it started to snow and snow and snow.

They were stranded with very little food. Fifteen members attempted to cross the daunting mountain range, but only eight made it to civilization at Sutter's Fort. The eight survivors had eaten their dead companions to survive. By the time the party was rescued in April 1847, it was apparent that those left at the camp had also resorted to eating their dead. In all, of the ninety-one Donner Party members, only forty-five survived, with at least twenty-five having turned to cannibalism.

The thirty-acre park nestled on the east bank of Donner Lake features scenic hiking trails with signs marking the locations of some of the Donner Party cabins. The Visitor Center houses the Emigrant Trail Museum, which focuses on the emigrant migration to the area, its Native Americans, and the area's involvement in the building of the transcontinental railroad. The Donner Party itself is noticeably downplayed, despite the grisly details of its members' fate being the real draw.

Pioneer Statue, Donner Memorial State Park

On the grounds is the Pioneer Monument dedicated to all those hearty emigrants who braved the daunting Sierra Nevada to reach California. Financed mostly by the Native Sons of the Golden West, who raised funds by selling salvaged pieces of wood from one of the Donner Party cabins, the statute is twenty-two feet high, the same height as the snow that piled during the winter of 1846.

TRUCKEE, CALIFORNIA:

Located five minutes from Donner Memorial State Park, this small, vibrant town has a historic downtown with no shortage of saloons. The town is also home to two small but worthwhile museums: Old Jail Museum (10142 Jibboon St.) and Truckee Railroad Museum (10075 Donner Pass Rd.).

VIRGINIA CITY, NEVADA:

Virginia City, Nevada

This Old West silver-mining town, only a half hour from Reno, is a lot of fun. Prominently featured on the old *Bonanza* TV series, this well-preserved town has plenty of Old West saloons, shops, museums, and restaurants. A young Samuel Clemens adopted the pen name 'Mark Twain' while writing for the Virginia City daily *Territorial Enterprise*.

WHERE CAN I WET MY WHISTLE?

OLD SACRAMENTO
River City Saloon, 916 2nd St., Sacramento, California

It's OK. It's in an old building that originally housed a brothel. It has pool tables now, along with a rowdy atmosphere.

River City Saloon, Old Sacramento

Sac Town Sports Bar & Grill, 106 J Street, Sacramento, California, (916)443-6852

It doesn't really fit in with the Old West theme, but the beer is cold.

PLACERVILLE
Liars' Bench, 255 Main St., Placerville, California

Nestled in this artsy-fartsy town is this true old man's dive bar serving cold tap beer in Mason jars.

Bucket of Blood Saloon, Virginia City

VIRGINIA CITY
Bucket of Blood Saloon, 1 South C Street, Virginia City, Nevada (775)847-0322

Housed in a circa 1876 building, the lively saloon drips with the Old West atmosphere and features live music on the weekends.

Ponderosa Saloon & Mine Tour, 106 South C Street, Virginia City, Nevada, (775)847-7210

How can you not go into an establishment named 'Ponderosa'? As bonus, they run a silver-mine tour out of the back of the bar. Cheers!

COLUMBIA

What Cheer Saloon, Columbia City Hotel, (209)532-1486

This establishment has been serving thirsty patrons from a beautiful cherrywood bar since 1857. You might even run into Mark Twain sipping a cocktail.

WHAT ABOUT GRUB?

PLACERVILLE

The Farm Table, 311 Main Street, Placerville, California, (530)295-8140

It serves great sandwiches on freshly baked bread. Try the daily sausage sandwich special served on a warm pretzel bun.

SACRAMENTO

The Firehouse Restaurant, 1112 Second Street, Sacramento, California, (916)442-4772

Located on the Old Sacramento waterfront, the restaurant is operated out of an old firehouse built in 1853 and serves up upscale American fare.

COLUMBIA

Christopher's at the City Hotel, 22768 Main Street, Columbia, California, (209)532-5964

Located in the historic hotel, this hotel serves the best burger in town.

TRUCKEE

Bar of America, 10040 Commercial Row at Bridge St., Truckee, California, (530)587-2626

This is the busiest place in town, offering generous portions of comfort food.

WHERE CAN I HANG MY HAT AND PUT MY BOOTS UNDER A BED?

SACRAMENTO

Being the state capital, Sacramento has no shortage of motels and hotels. If Sacramento is your base of operations, I recommend the following.

Holiday Inn, 300 J. Street, Sacramento, (916)445-0100)

It's a Holiday Inn, but it's a short walk to Old Sacramento. It's also located right next to a mall that has a Yard House with over a hundred beers on tap.

PLACERVILLE

Carey House Hotel, 300 Main Street, Placerville, (530)622-4271)

A historic boutique hotel whose former famous guests have run the gamut from Mark Twain and U.S. Grant to Elvis Presley and Bette Davis.

COLUMBIA

The Columbia City Hotel, 22768 Main Street, Columbia, California, (209)532-5964 and Hotel Fallon, 11175 Washington St., (209)532-1470

Columbia City Hotel

Both are restored early-nineteenth-century inns located on the state park grounds.

Hotel Fallon, Columbia City California

WHAT SHOULD I WATCH AND READ BEFORE I HIT THE TRAIL?

BOOKS

- *The Forty-Niners* (1974, Time-Life Series, The Old West)—an easy read with scores of excellent photographs
- *Days of Gold: The California Gold Rush and the American Nation* (1997, by Malcolm J. Rohrbough)—a comprehensive review of the California gold rush and its historical impact
- *The Age of Gold: The California Gold Rush and the New American Dream* (2002, by H.W. Brands)—the gold rush years as seen through the eyes of diverse participants, including John and Jessie Fremont

VIDEOS

- *California* (1947, Paramount DVD)—Ray Milland stars as an army deserter who heads a wagon train bound for California during the gold rush. The film also features scene-stealing Barry Fitzgerald.
- *American Experience: The Gold Rush* (2006, PBS DVD)—a detailed review of the gold rush years, with an emphasis on its negative impacts on the environment and Native Americans.

TIPS FROM THE TRAIL

A good base of operations is either Sacramento or Reno or a combination of both. You can spend a full day in Old Sacramento, which offers plenty of lodging, dining, and drinking options. It is only about an hour away from Sutter's Mill. From the vibrant Reno, you are only a half hour from Truckee, California, Donner State Park, and Virginia City.

California's First Millionaire

Sam Brannan (Library of Congress, LC-USZ62-49618)

Like most, if not all, people who found themselves in far-flung California in 1848, Sam Brannan was something of a character. Born in Maine, he moved around New England working in various capacities, including as a journalist and land speculator before becoming, of all things, an elder of a Mormon Church in New York. In 1846, to escape persecution by the Mormons, he led his flock on a venture to Mexican California to establish a colony far from American prejudices. After an arduous six-month sea voyage around Cape Horn, the Saints arrived at Yerba Buena (San Francisco) only to discover U.S. troops already occupied the port. Although the Mexican-American War was not yet officially over, an American victory seemed to be a foregone conclusion. Despite California no longer being a foreign refuge, Brannan still felt California had enough positive attributes to make it a suitable location for the church.

He set out east to Utah, crossing the Sierra Nevada, to convince Mormon leader Brigham Young that the fertile lands of California were a more suitable location for their church than the Great Salt Lake Basin. Young wasn't having it, or Brannan either. The disappointed Brannan left for California no longer an elder in the Church of Latter Day Saints. He was a little richer though, since he never turned over to the Mormon leader the tithe he had collected from the church's members. In fact, Brannan continued tithing when he returned to California. When Young heard about it, he sent an envoy to California to collect the donations. The envoy returned to the Salt Lake Basin empty-handed, having been told by Brannan, "You go back and tell Brigham Young that I'll give up the Lord's money when he sends me a receipt signed by the Lord." The hard-drinking Brannan was ultimately ex-communicated.

As fate would have it, he arrived back at Sutter's Fort just as Marshall was starting construction of the mill, and so he set up a store within the walls of the fort to sell supplies and provisions for the mill's construction, as well as for Sutter's other ventures. Consequently, he was one of the first people to hear of Marshall's incredible discovery and to confirm the talk of gold, when mill workers started using gold dust to pay for purchases made in his store, which mostly consisted of liquor. Brannan promptly, and correctly, surmised he could make more money selling supplies to miners than he could panning for gold. He just needed to drum up customers.

He filled a quinine bottle with gold dust and paraded through the streets of San Francisco, boisterously shouting, "Gold! Gold! Gold from the American River!" San Francisco emptied out, and Brannan was in business. He bought out all the supplies in San Francisco and established another store next to Sutter's Mill. Gold pans he bought for twenty cents he sold for eight dollars each; shovels sold for thirty-five dollars, equal to a thousand dollars today. His stores were grossing five thousand dollars, the equivalent of a hundred twenty thousand dollars, per day in today's dollars.

Brannan continued to prosper through the 1850s into the 1860s. He owned many buildings in San Francisco and Sacramento and purchased land in Napa Valley, Hawaii, and Southern California. He lived a lavish lifestyle, traveled widely, and was referred to as the richest man in California. But by the 1870s he was spreading himself too thin. His drinking steadily increased, and his business judgment decreased. He got divorced along the way, and his ex-wife took him to the cleaners. The final straw was a bad business deal in Mexico that compensated him with land that turned out worthless. When he died in 1889, his second wife did not have enough money to bury him.

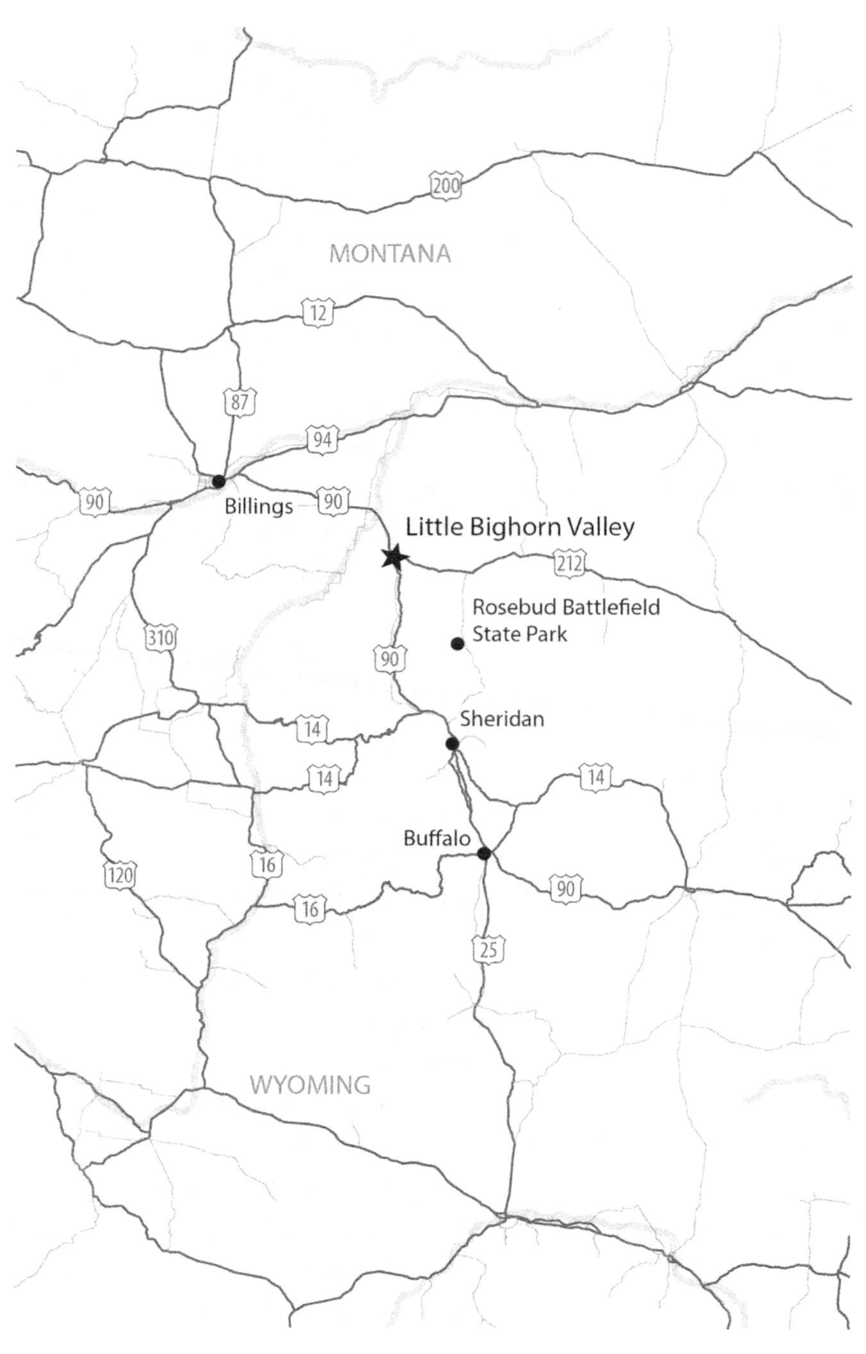

MONTANA
200
12
87
94
90
Billings
90
Little Bighorn Valley
212
Rosebud Battlefield
State Park
310
90
14
Sheridan
14
14
Buffalo
120
16
90
16
25
WYOMING

Little Bighorn Valley

Montana

Battle of Little Bighorn (Library of Congress, Digital ID 3b53143)

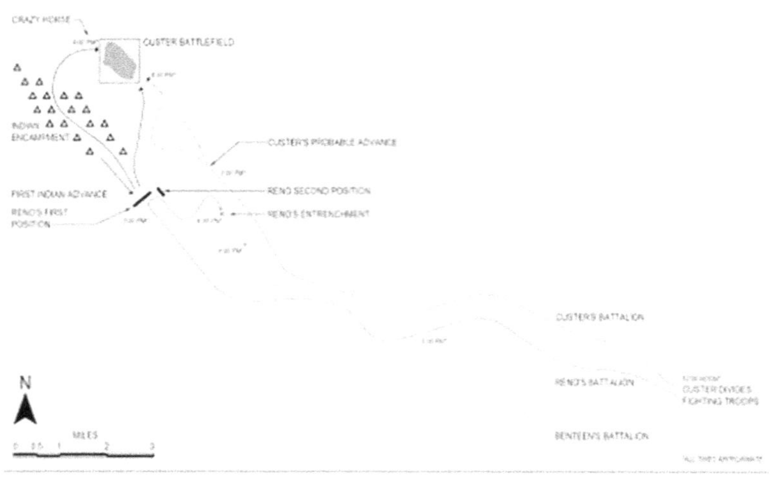

WHAT HAPPENED HERE?

On June 25, 1876, on the sloping grassy banks of the Little Bighorn River, the seemingly indestructible, and media darling, the dashing Lt. Col. George Armstrong Custer, and his entire command of two hundred and sixty-eight men, including his brother, brother-in-law, and nephew were wiped out by an overwhelming number of Lakota Sioux, Northern Cheyenne, and Arapaho warriors, under Chief Sitting Bull.

The country's most renowned Indian fighter, although vastly outnumbered, had, somewhat inexplicably, led a charge into the largest encampment of Indians ever assembled in North America, with unprecedented and disastrous results.

The seeds of the debacle had been sewn two years earlier when the Army was dispatched into the Black Hills of Western Dakota to supposedly scout for a location for a military fort. The fly in the buttermilk was that the Black Hills were located in the Sioux reservation, and the unstated objective for the exhibition was to confirm persistent rumors that there was gold in them thar hills. Ironically, it was none other than Custer and his 7th Calvary that were sent into the Black Hills, and returned touting

George Armstrong Custer (Library of Congress, LC DIG-03110)

that gold was plentiful, and was even 'among the roots of the grass'. The Country was in the midst of a monetary depression, and newspaper headlines promptly predicted a new gold rush: 'GOLD'; 'Prepare for Lively Times!' Thousands of prospectors, and the assorted lot of characters (gamblers, soiled doves, con-men, etc.) that follow them, started pouring into the sacred lands of the Sioux. The Army simply could not keep them out. Efforts to purchase the Black Hills from the Sioux failed, and the enraged Sioux were consolidating and becoming more combative. Something had to be done.

In the spring of 1876, General Philip Sheridan devised a strategy for 2500 troopers to converge on the region in Montana Territory containing the Powder, Rosebud, Bighorn, and Yellowstone rivers; a known summer gathering spot of the Lakota Cheyenne people. To force the Sioux out of the gold-laden Black Hills, and onto reservations, Sheridan ordered a three-prong attack. Colonel John Gibbon, from Fort Ellis in Montana, would head west, Gen. George Crook would head north from Fort Fetterman in Wyoming, and General Alfred Terry, along with Lt. Col. George Custer, and the 7th Calvary would push east, from Fort Abraham Lincoln in Dakota Territory.

General Phillip Sheridan (standing) with his Civil War generals (Custer is seated on the right). (Library of Congress LC-88184)

Crook met Indian resistance on the banks of the Rosebud Creek, in Montana Territory, and, simply, turned around, and went back to Wyoming. The planned three-prong attack was now a two-prong attack. Gibbon and Terry did rendezvous at the Yellowstone River, on the steamship, Far West, and they concluded that the elusive Indians were, indeed, in the Little Bighorn Valley. Gen. Terry ordered Custer to take his command to the Little Bighorn Valley from the south, and Gibbon was to approach from the other direction.

Custer, pushing his men relentlessly, got there first, and he wasn't about to wait. He didn't need any other of the prongs. He was so sure of the superiority of his men that he had demurred on taking three Gatling guns, yet another blunder by the over-confident commander. Over 10,000 Sioux and Cheyenne had gathered by the Little Bighorn River, and under the guidance of the revered spiritual leader, Sitting Bull, the warriors had pledged to resist.

A few weeks earlier, Sitting Bull had a vision of soldiers falling into his camp; a prediction that the bluecoats would attack, and be killed. On the morning of June 25, Custer's advance scouts, from about fifteen miles away spotted a large Indian encampment near the Little Bighorn River. Custer, fearing that he may have been spotted and that his prey would scatter, demurred on resting his weary troops, and immediately made plans for an attack on the village.

Despite the scout's warning of an immense Indian village, Custer, nonetheless, divided his command into three segments: one hundred and twenty-five men, under the able leadership of Captain Frederick Benteen, were to stay with the pack train

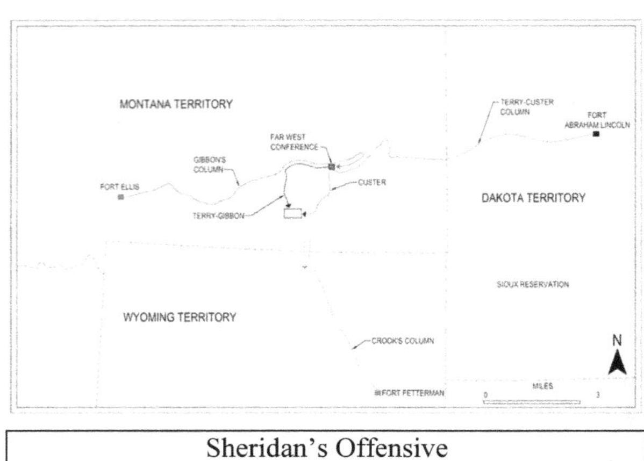

Sheridan's Offensive

loaded with ammunition and supplies, scout the hills to the west, and 'pitch into' any Indians they encountered; one hundred and forty men commanded by Major Marcus Reno were ordered to cross the river and strike the southern end of the village, about two miles away; and Custer with two hundred and twenty men would march to the hills north of the village. Since his command was ultimately annihilated, and he chose not to explain his orders to his subordinates, Custer's overall tactical strategy is still debated among history buffs. There is no debating, however, that whatever his plan was; it didn't work.

Things rapidly started falling apart, when, as soon as Reno, crossed the

Major Marcus Reno (Denver Public Library)

river, he met unexpected and heavy Indian resistance. Reno immediately halted the attack and set up a defensive skirmish line in a wooded area. While in the timber, Reno was trying to gather himself, and vainly looking for support from Custer, when a bullet struck an Indian scout, Bloody Knife, in the head, splattering blood, brains, and gore all over the already shaken Reno. Reno lost it. All thoughts of attacking the Village were gone, and Reno and his panicked command, beat a hasty and undisciplined retreat to a high bluff, on the other side of the river, henceforth known as Reno Hill, suffering heavy casualties.

Miles away, blissfully unaware of Reno's unfolding rout, Custer rode northward along the bluffs, where for the first time he laid eyes on the thousands of teepees, across the river. He was elated, yelling to his men, "We've got them this time!" Through his adjutant Lieutenant W.W. Cooke, Custer sent a message to Benteen. Scrawled on a piece of paper, and handed to Trumpeter Giovanni Martini, the arguably contractionary message read: "Benteen. Come on. Big village—be quick—bring packs. W.W. Cooke P.S. bring pacs."

Bugler Giovanni Martini, aka John Martin (Denver Public Library)

Benteen received the note and quickened his pace toward the Little Bighorn. He joined Reno on the bluffs, who insisted that Benteen, remain on Reno Hill; "For God's sake, Benteen, halt your command and help me. I've lost half my men." Custer was now on his own.

Having thwarted Reno's half-hearted attack, the emboldened warriors turned their full attention to the doomed Custer. Led by Crazy Horse, and Sioux Chief Gall, as many as a thousand warriors crossed the Little Bighorn, stormed up the hill, and clashed with Custer, on the Western slope of Custer Hill, just below where the present monument stands. On that very spot, Custer, and what was left of his command, made their 'last stand' of legend and lore. Ultimately, forty-two bodies, including Custer, and his brothers Tom, and Boston were located behind a barricade of dead horses.

For the next two days, Reno and Benteen held off sporadic Indian attacks until Gen. Terry finally arrived. Capt. Benteen has been credited with saving the day, having taken control from the rattled and sometimes intoxicated, Major Reno. On June 27, the surviving troopers of the 7th Calvary came upon the ghastly, surreal, scene of the demise of Custer's command. After two days baking in the summer sun, the grossly mutilated bodies of their fellow soldiers were quickly buried in shallow graves. Custer's body was spared mutilation, prompting speculation that it was a gesture of respect by his opponents.

Sitting Bull (Library of Congress, LC-DIG 39879

WHAT HAPPENED NEXT?

The shocking news reached the East on July 5, 1876, as the young country was in the midst of its Centennial celebration. Newspapers accounts were quick to assess blame for the 'massacre'. Custer did not entirely escape criticism for his seemingly foolhardy actions, but the papers painted the real villains as the US Army, and President U.S. Grant for placing America's most famous Indian fighter in harm's way. Grant was limping through the last scandal-ridden year of his presidency, and was an easy mark. Grant responded that Custer's action was 'foolhardy'. There was no love lost between Custer and his Commander-in-Chief (see p. 93).

Sitting Bull also received a lot of ink, which, surprisingly, sympathetically portrayed him as a sage Indian Chief, and a tactical genius on a par with Napoleon. Actually, Sitting Bull was considered by his people as a spiritual leader, who did not take an active role in the battle. The driving force among the warriors was actually the enigmatic Crazy Horse, a devilish site, with his chest and arms covered off with painted white hailstone totems, and a yellow-painted lightning bolt down the middle of his face. He charged fearlessly toward the soldiers, believing his medicine made him immune from enemy bullets.

There was enough blame to go around. Major Marcus Reno, although salvaging his command, thanks to the capable assistance of Captain Benteen, came under heavy criticism for not coming to his commander's aid. Reno demanded a military court of inquiry, which ultimately cleared him of any wrongdoing.

Clearly, Custer's devastating defeat had to be avenged. The full weight of the US Army was brought down on the Sioux. Within a year, most of the Sioux were on reservations, and Crazy Horse was dead. Sitting Bull slipped away to Canada, but returned to the States, in 1881 with about two hundred forlorn followers and finally surrendered. He would spend the rest of his life on reservations but was occasionally permitted to travel, even performing for a season with Buffalo Bill's Wild West show. He was killed at the Standing Rock reservation on December 15, 1890, triggered by government fears that the still influential leader was part of the controversial Ghost Dance movement.

George and his devoted Libbie during the Civil War years (Library of Congress, LC-BH831-702)

A year after the massacre, the remnants of the 7th Cavalry undertook the arduous task of exhuming the remains of Custer, eleven other officers, and two civilians, for reinternment elsewhere. Custer was re buried, with much military pomp and circumstance at the Post Cemetery at the US Military Academy, West Point, NY. Custer's beloved Libby, who would remain a widow for fifty-six years, was in attendance, as was the lucky trumpeter, Giovanni Martini, who played Taps. Libby would go on to write three books on her experiences in the West, and would dedicate her long life to preserving and safeguarding the memory of her beloved 'Autie'.

Marking where Lt. Crittenden fell, c. 1879 (Library of Congress, LC-USZ62-51708)

In 1879, soldiers, once again, returned to exhume the slain troopers' bodies from their hastily dug graves for reburial at the top of Custer Hill. The battlefield was designated a National Cemetery, and in 1881 the granite monument, still standing today, was erected. In 1946, the Custer Battlefield National Cemetery was renamed Custer Battlefield National Monument, and management transferred from the War Department to the National Park Service.

In August 1983, a fire swept through the battlefield, stripping away decades of prairie grass and thick underbrush. Although initially perceived to be a disaster, the fire actually exposed the battlefield surface to such an extent that archaeologists were able to recover over 5000 artifacts, as well as human remains. Encouraged by these tantalizing finds, historians have continued to analyze the weapons utilized by both sides, as well as the chronology of the battle. Based on the location and amount of ammunition casings that were unearthed, students of the battle now believe that the Indians had more firepower than was previously

Native American Memorial

thought. The excavations, also confirmed that Custer Hill, was, indeed, the site of a 'last stand'.

As the decades passed, it finally came to light that, the Indians, also, had their side of the story to tell. In addition to the museum making a concentrated effort to display artifacts depicting the Indian's vanishing culture, in 1992 the name of the park was again changed to Little Bighorn National Monument. In 1999, red granite markers were added to the battlefield to denote where Indian warriors fell, and Indian memorials were added in 2003 and 2013. It was a long time coming, but the overall effect is to give the visitor a more balanced perspective, on not only what occurred on this still desolate spot, but the heavy price the Indians ultimately paid for their victory.

Thanks, in large part to the efforts of his widow, George Armstrong Custer would come to be perceived as a martyr to Manifest Destiny, and Custer's Last Stand a heroic battle in which the 7th Calvary, despite overwhelming odds chose to fight to the last man, rather than surrender. Buffalo Bill Cody's Wild West show's reenactment of Custer's Last Stand was a crowd favorite for decades. Custer would be a popular subject for books and movies for the next hundred years; predominately portrayed as the flamboyant soldier, destined for glory on Last Stand Hill.

The actions of Custer and his officers' actions on that hot June day in 1876 continue to spark debate among historians and history buffs. Did Custer disobey orders by not waiting for Gen. Gibbon? Did Custer make a monumental blunder by dividing his command, in the face of an overwhelming superior force? Did Reno fail his Commander by not pressing his attack on the village? Were both Reno and Benteen derelict in their duties for not coming to Custer's aid? Despite Custer's image having lost some of its luster, these controversies have kept the Battle of the Little Bighorn as the most popular subject of the Western print genre, and Custer's name is, hands down, the most recognizable associated with the Old West. At a 2018 Heritages Auction, collectors plunked down over a million dollars for artifacts associated with Custer and his final battle. Fifty or so strands of the Boy General's hair sold for $10,000 and three Sioux arrows, recovered from the battlefield went for a whopping $75,000! In 2017, a gun collector paid $400,000 for an 1873 Colt authenticated to have been carried by one of Custer's men. Americans are still fascinated with George Armstrong Custer, and his spectacular demise a century and a half ago, on the banks of the Little Bighorn River.

WHAT DO I DO WHEN I GET THERE?

Little Bighorn National Monument, 756 Battlefield Tour Rd., Crow Agency, MT 59022, (405)638-3216

Administered by the National Park Service, the battlefield site attracts 300,000 visitors a year. The Visitor Center offers a twenty-five-minute film explaining the battle, and the museum displays numerous military and Indian artifacts associated with the participants, including Sitting Bull's moccasins and Custer's fringed buckskin jacket.

Little Bighorn Memorial

From Memorial Day through Labor Day Park Rangers give five 40-minute talks on various aspects of the battle and its aftermath. Visitors can take a self-guiding 4.5 mile audio driving tour that starts at the Reno Benteen Battlefield and ends at the Visitor Center. Marble markers, ostensibly showing where the soldier's bodies were found and initially buried are scattered throughout the landscape. The highlight of the tour is Custer Hill, on the western slope of the northern end of Battle Ridge, where what was left of Custer's command made their last stand. An iron fence encloses the fifty-two tightly grouped markers, including that of Lt. Col. Custer. A Memorial Monument, erected in 1881 stands at the top of the hill marking the final resting place of the slain troopers.

The battlefield site also encompasses the Custer National Cemetery, in which over 5000 Veterans, and their dependents are buried.

Guided tours, are also available through Apsaalooke Tours. (406) 6383897. A mini-coach leaves from the Visitor Center five times daily, hosted by Native Americans, who give a unique perspective on the battle. Private tours are also available, by appointment.

Garyowen, Montana

IS THERE ANYTHING ELSE?

Garryowen, Montana, Frontage Rd. (I-90, Exit 514)

The privately owned town, named after the old Irish pub tune adopted by the 7th Calvary as their marching song, is physically located on the site of Sitting Bull's camp. The seven-acre parcel is home to the Custer Battlefield Museum. The impressive museum has a diverse collection of artifacts, including a lock of Custer's hair, the death mask of Sitting Bull, and a revolver owned by Tom Custer. The privately owned artifacts have been valued at over four million dollars. An interesting side note is that in 2005 some of the artifacts were confiscated by the Federal Bureau of Land Management in a raid premised on the allegation of dealing in fraudulent artifacts. Although no formal charges were ever brought, it took over a decade for the seized items to be returned.

In 1926, during highway construction, the skull of a US Calvary trooper was unearthed, and subsequently buried in the Tomb of the Unknown Soldier, the only such site not located in a National Cemetery.

After years of trying to sell the town, in 2018, the owner finally gave up and announced plans to build a world-class museum and research center.

A little over an hour south of the Little Bighorn, is the site of June 17, 1876 battle, when Gen. Crook was surprised by Cheyenne and Lakota warriors, on his way north to hook up with Custer. He never made it. The sides were pretty evenly matched, at about 1000 combatants each. The battle lasted about six hours, but, despite the fierce fighting, casualties were light, with only about forty killed on both sides.

Rosebud Battlefield

Under the leadership of Crazy Horse and Sitting Bull, Crook's forces were forced to withdraw. The wounded were brought back to Fort Fetterman, and Crook, along with some of his officers went on a fishing trip. Eight days later Custer would meet his fate, without any assistance from Crook. The General's somewhat lackadaisical attempt to rendezvous with Custer has subjected him to historical criticism, and one can't help but wonder what would have happened at the Little Bighorn, had Crook showed up with a thousand troops.

The State Park, which is located off a desolate Route 314 is disappointing. Most of the ten square miles of battlefield is on private farmland and is not accessible. There are no signs, memorials, or buildings. What the Park does provide are a picnic table, a tiny kiosk holding brochures, and three bronze plaques describing the battle. However, similar to the Little Bighorn, the landscape remains as it was at the time of the battle, with sloping grassy ridges. For that reason alone, it's worth the trip.

WHERE CAN I WET MY WHISTLE?

Well, you're on an Indian Reservation, so, if you're hankering for firewater, your best bet is in **Billings**, Montana, or **Wyoming**.

The Mint Bar, 151 N. Main Street, Sheridan, Wyoming

Built in 1907, it is Sheridan's oldest bar and managed to survive Prohibition by operating as a speakeasy. Great atmosphere; the walls are decorated with dead animals and branding irons.

The Bozeman Trail Inn, 158 Johnson St., Big Horn, Wyoming

Located about ten miles south of Sheridan, this 1882 watering hole was an oasis for thirsty travelers along the Bozeman Trail.

Mint Bar

WHAT ABOUT GRUB?

Custer Battlefield Trading Post and Café, 347 Highway 212 (Exit 510 I90), Crow Agency, Montana

Located right across the battlefield. The only game in town, but it's pretty good. It's hooked up with a Trading Post, in which you could kill an hour, rummaging through the souvenirs, artifacts, books, and Indian arts and crafts. Try the Indian Taco.

WHERE CAN I HANG MY HAT AND PUT MY BOOTS UNDER A BED?

The only accommodations close to the battlefield are a couple of RV campsites.

- The 7th Ranch RV Camp, 514 Reno Creek Rd, Garryowen, Montana, (406)638-2438)

It also has some small cabins for rent. About fifteen miles away is the small town (emphasis on small), of Hardin, Montana, which has some nondescript two-and three-star motels.

- Lariat Motel, 709 N. Center Ave., Hardin, Montana, (406)665-2683
- Rodeway Inn, 1324 N. Crawford Ave., Hardin, Montana, (406)665-1870

Your best bet, depending on which direction you're heading to, or coming from is to stay either in Billings, Montana, hundred miles north, or in Sheridan, Wyoming, about seventy miles south of the Little Bighorn.

Also, Buffalo, Wyoming, about hundred miles south is a good option.

SHERIDAN

Sheridan Inn, 856 Broadway Street, Sheridan, Wyoming, (307)6742178 (sheridaninn.com)

Among the first owners, was none other than Buffalo Bill Cody, who, in 1873, saw the opportunity for an inn on the railroad line. Each of the twenty-two rooms focuses on Buffalo Bill, and his colorful contemporaries through art, photos, and artifacts. It has a great front porch and the original bar.

BILLINGS

Northern Hotel, 19 North Broadway, Billings, Montana

Opened in 1904, although the original building burned down in 1940. It was rebuilt as the most luxurious hotel in Billings; which it remains.

Dude Rancher Lodge, 415 N. 29th Street, (406)545-0121

Built in the 1950s TV Western heyday, it has maintained its kitschy nostalgic atmosphere, despite going through several renovations.

BUFFALO

Occidental Hotel, 10 N. Main Street, Buffalo, Wyoming

About an hour and a half away, off I90, is the small, historic town of Buffalo, Wyoming, home to one of the best authentic hotels of the Old West, the Occidental. It's worth the side trip, just to see the hotel, but you should really spend the night. Built in 1880, the Occidental has hosted a virtual who's who of the Old West: Buffalo Bill Cody, Gen. Phil Sheridan, Tom Horn, Calamity Jane, Teddy Roosevelt, and Butch Cassidy, and the Sundance Kid,

Lobby of Occidental Hotel

whose infamous Hole in the Wall hideout is a short drive away. Stepping into the saloon is like going back in time a hundred years, and there is a nightly country and Western musical entertainment. The rooms and suites are themed and are decorated accordingly. *The Bordello* is my favorite. The renowned author, Owen Wister spent a considerable amount of time at the hotel, so the on-premises steakhouse is aptly named after his classic, *The Virginian*.

The saloon at the Occidental.

WHAT SHOULD I WATCH AND READ BEFORE I HIT THE TRAIL?

BOOKS

- *The Custer Reader* (1992, edited by renowned historian Dr. Paul Andrew Hutton)—everything you ever wanted to know about George Armstrong Custer.
- *A Terrible Glory. Custer and the Little Bighorn. The Last Great Battle of the American West* (2008), by James Donovan—Highly detailed, but easily readable analysis of the battle. *Custer: The*

Controversial Life of George Armstrong Custer (1996), by Jeffry D. Wert—an exhaustive biography of the controversial Custer.

VIDEOS

- *They Died With Their Boots On* (1941)—Errol Flynn is the dashing Custer, in this sentimental, but rousing portrayal of the Last Stand.
- *Little Big Man* (1970)—Dustin Hoffman is the 121 old Jack Crabb who recalls his life on the Western frontier, including his survival of the Little Big Horn. Richard Mulligan's Custer is a self-absorbed somewhat crazy commander.
- *Son of the Morning Star* (1991)—This is a made-for-TV movie that is more historically accurate than most.

TIPS FROM THE TRAIL

The Little Bighorn Battlefield is a must-see for any Wild West enthusiast. The locale is almost unchanged from 1876, unlike other historic sites (the Alamo, Dodge City), in which civilization has infringed to such an extent, that it is difficult to visualize how the locale looked over a century ago. However, since the twenty-first century hasn't caught up with the Little Bighorn, it's a day trip, on your way to somewhere else. Usually, during the third week of June, there is a Little Bighorn Battle reenactment, in nearby Hardin, Montana.

Captain Benteen (Denver Public Library)

Custer almost did not meet his destiny at the Little Bighorn. Affectionately referred to as the 'Boy General' for the Civil War heroics that prompted his meteoric rise to Brevet major general at the age of 23, in the post-war Army, he held the rank of Lt. Colonel, but his men still referred to him as 'General'. However, Custer's military career had not been without its setbacks. He had been court-martialed twice and had spent the spring of 1876 back east trying to re-establish his command of the 7th Calvary after he had been relieved from duty by President Grant. Grant, who was limping through the last scandal-ridden year of his presidency, was infuriated with Custer's testimony before a Congressional Committee that had implicated the President's brother Orvile in irregularities in the handling of Indian Post Traderships.

While Generals Sherman, Sheridan, and Terry interceded on his behalf, Custer cooled his heels in New York and Philadelphia, where he took in the

Philadelphia Exposition and would boast that his 7th Calvary could 'whip and defeat all the Indians on the plains'.

In April 1876, Grant relented, and Custer re-joined his Command at Fort Abraham Lincoln, in time for the ill-fated summer campaign to whip all the Indians on the Montana plains. Not everybody in the 7th Calvary was happy to see the return of Custer. In particular Captain Frederick Benteen, whose dislike of his commander bordered on hatred. Benteen was openly critical of Custer's actions, eight years prior, at the 1868 Battle of the Washita, in which Benteen claimed that he 'abandoned' Major Joel Elliot, and his men during the conflict.

Custer also drove his men hard, and his inner circle within the officer corps was largely made up of his family and friends. Benteen was not in the inner circle, and neither was his second-in-command, Major Reno. It has long been debated, among Little Bighorn buffs, if Reno and Benteen's dislike of Custer influenced their actions during the battle, in not coming to their commander's aid.

Although Reno's military career survived the Court of Inquiry in 1879, he was never the same. His drinking, which had been on a steady increase after his wife's death in 1874, spiraled out of control, after the Little Bighorn. In 1880, he was accused of peeping into the window of the daughter of his commanding officer. Not good. He was dishonorably discharged and died of cancer in 1889.

Benteen's reputation didn't take the hit that Reno's did, but he also had a weakness for the bottle, not an uncommon problem in the nineteenth-century military. Although promoted to Major in 1883, in 1887, he was court-martialed for drunkenness and conduct unbecoming an officer and gentleman, and was suspended from the service for a year. He came back a year later but was promptly discharged for medical reasons. In 1892, he was ceremoniously promoted to Brigadier General for 'gallant and meritorious service' at the Little Bighorn.

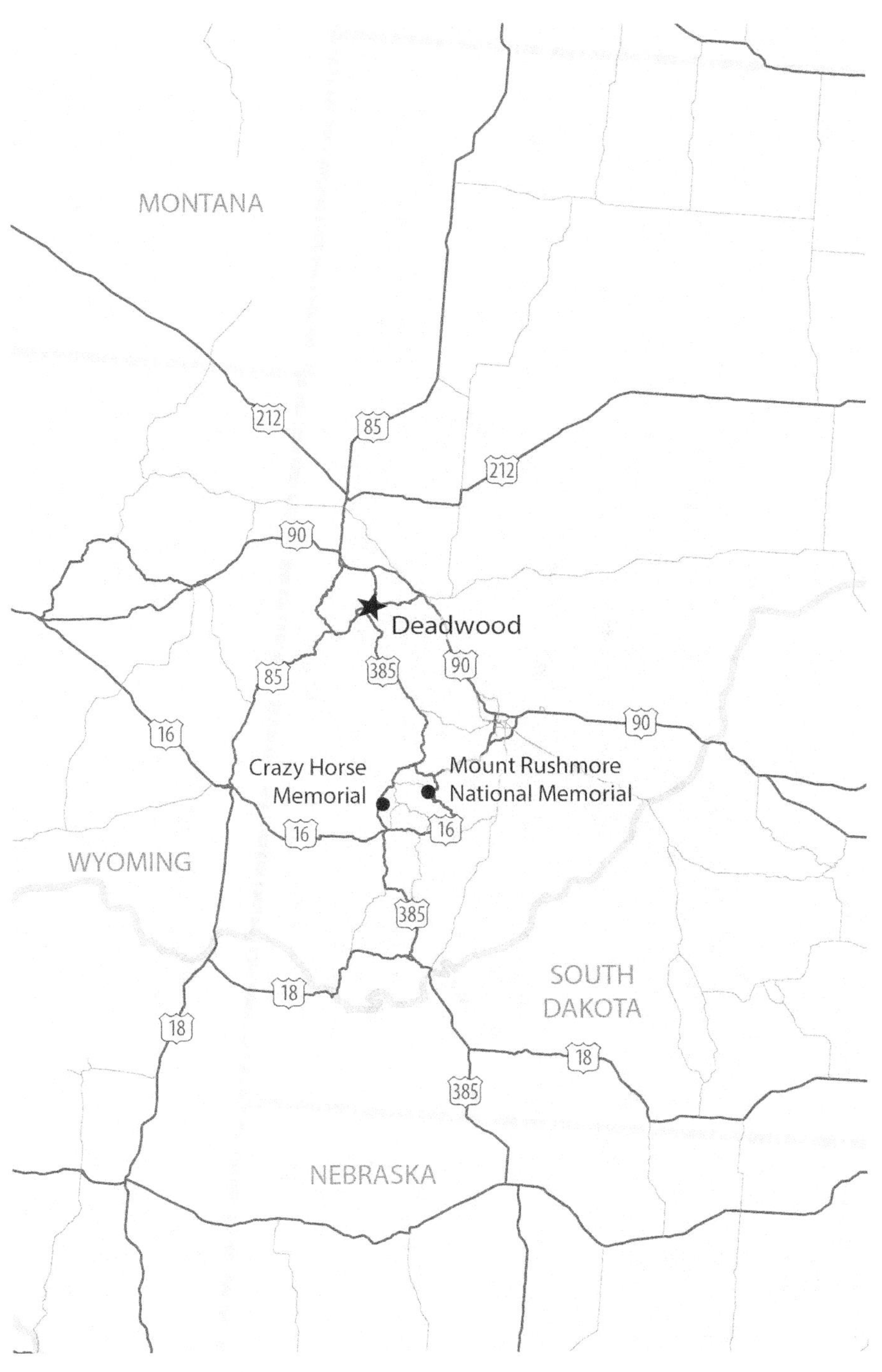

MONTANA
212
85
212
90
85
Deadwood
385
90
85
90
16
Crazy Horse
Memorial
Mount Rushmore
National Memorial
16
16
WYOMING
385
SOUTH
DAKOTA
18
18
18
385
NEBRASKA

Deadwood

South Dakota

Deadwood, 1875 (Courtesy Black Hills State University)

WHAT HAPPENED HERE?

On the afternoon of August 2, 1876, James Butler, 'Wild Bill' Hickok was playing poker at Nuttal and Mann's No. 10 Saloon, on the Main Street of the rapidly growing mining town of Deadwood, Dakota Territory, when twenty-five-year-old Jack McCall, walked a few feet behind Hickok, drew his six-shooter, and fired one shot into the back of the famed gunfighter's head, killing him instantly.

For a hundred years prior, the Black Hills of what now encompasses 4,500 square miles in Southwestern South Dakota and Eastern Wyoming was sacred land to the Lakota Sioux. The fierce warriors had seized the bountiful land from the rival Cheyenne in 1776 and kept it. The craggy mountains were called Paha' Sapa, or 'Hills That Are Black', because, from a distance, the dense Ponderosa Pines, and dark rock formations, make the mountains appear to be black.

Rumors of gold had been luring white men to the Black Hills since the 1830s, but the tenacious Sioux had been successful in warding off would-be miners and rival tribes for decades. The Sioux thought that their trespassing problem was permanently resolved with the signing of the Treaty of Laraime in 1868, which provided that the cherished Black Hills was 'for the absolute and undisturbed use and occupancy of the Sioux'. White man speaks with forked tongue.

In 1874, Lt. Col. George Armstrong Custer, a lightning rod for controversy, marched a thousand troopers into the Black Hills. His mission was to scout a site for a new army fort, to ostensibly assist the Sioux in keeping out unwanted white settlers. Complicating this already twisted military logic was that his secondary objective was to assess the reliability of the persistent Black Hills gold rumors. Custer confirmed that, indeed, there was gold in the Black Hills, and to ensure that the word spread quickly, as was his custom, he had brought along newspaper reporters on his foray into Dakota Territory. Fanning the flames of gold hysteria, Custer pronounced that the Black Hills were on a par with 'the richest regions in Colorado'. The gold rush was on, with over 10,000 miners descending upon the Sioux's ancestral hunting grounds, within a year.

In 1875, a miner discovered gold, in a narrow canyon, in the Black Hills, laden with dead trees, and christened the site 'Deadwood Gulch', and the boomtown quickly had a population of somewhere between 5000 and 10,000 with another 25,000 prospectors roaming the nearby hills. Initially, the mining camp was a hodgepodge of hastily built structures and tents, with no shortage of saloons, and brothels. By the summer of 1876, more permanent wooden structures sprang up, housing almost two hundred businesses, and over a million dollars of gold, at twenty dollars an ounce, had been mined from the region. Since Deadwood was illegally founded on Sioux land, no government authority existed, so it truly was a lawless, dangerous settlement. It was oft repeated that a murder a day occurred in Deadwood.

In July 1876, Colorado Charlie Utter drove a wagon train of about hundred fortune seekers into town, which included in its number, two Wild West icons who would forever be linked to each other, as well as to Deadwood: 'Wild Bill' Hickok, and Mary 'Calamity Jane' Canary.

Deadwood Main Street, 1878 (Black Hills State University)

Wild Bill rolled into town the most famous gunfighter alive. Buffalo hunter, Army scout, lawman, romanticized hero of countless dime novels, friends to George Custer, and Buffalo Bill, the dashing Hickok, however, was an 'old' thirty-nine-years old. He had hung up his badge five years earlier, when he had accidentally shot and killed his deputy marshal during a gunfight in Abilene, Kansas. His eyesight was decreasing, his drinking increasing, and he had a bad feeling about Deadwood, confiding to Colorado Charlie that he sensed that 'this is going to be my last camp'. Oddly, the lifelong bachelor had finally tied the knot, just four months prior, marrying a former circus performer, Agnes Lake, who was eleven years his senior. Despite his pessimism, he hoped, at long last, to find his elusive fortune, send for his new bride, and settle down. It was not to be.

Calamity Jane (National Archives)

The rough-and-tumble buckskin-clad Calamity Jane rolled into town, a hot mess. Although only twenty-four years old, she had already led a full life: laundress and camp follower of military expeditions in the Dakota Territory (including Custer's), ox-team driver, dance hall girl, and, of course, a prostitute. Topping off her unique rough-hewn masculine personality was the fact that she was a raging alcoholic.

Wild Bill's short stay in Deadwood came to an abrupt and bloody end on the afternoon of August 2, 1876. As was becoming his custom, Hickok, sought refuge from the stifling mid-day heat, in Nuttal and Mann's No. 10 Saloon, a wood timber building only about twenty feet in length, situated on the lower end of Main Street. After grabbing an adult beverage, at the bar, the nattily dressed Wild Bill joined a poker game, reluctantly taking the only available seat, which was near the rear entrance, facing the front entrance. The savvy gunslinger preferred to sit with his back to the wall, giving him a view of both entrances.

He even asked one of the players to move, so he could have his regular seat but was turned down. As the game progressed the uncomfortable Hickok, once again asked to switch seats, but the gambler still refused. It has been speculated that the famous Wild Bill's requests being summarily denied, was an indication of how far his star had fallen by the time he reached Deadwood. In any event, the seat selection would have a fatal consequence. Unnoticed by the card players, at about 4:00 pm a young drifter, named Jack McCall, entered through the front entrance, and made his way over to the bar.

He walked along the length of the bar until he made his way directly behind Hickok's chair. Standing just a few feet away from the preoccupied Hickok, McCall drew his six-shooter and fired a shot into the back of the gunfighter's head. The bullet passed through Hickok's skull, and exited through his right cheek, striking another gambler in the wrist. Hickok was killed instantly and fell sideways unto the floor. Dropping unto the table from his lifeless hands were pairs of Eights and Aces, henceforth known as the 'dead man's hand'.

Wild Bill Hickok (National Archives)

McCall threatened the stunned bar patrons, waving, and even attempting to fire his revolver; but it misfired. He scurried out the back door, into the alley behind the building, but didn't get too far. Hearing the shot, a crowd had gathered on Main Street, and the assassin was soon captured in a nearby butcher shop. Barely escaping a lynch mob, McCall was tried the very next day, and incredibly found not guilty. McCall's successful defense was that he had killed Wild Bill because the gunfighter had killed his brother; which wasn't true.

However, the trial was declared 'illegal', since Deadwood was actually located on an Indian Reservation, so the hastily convened 'miners court' did not have jurisdiction to adjudicate criminal offenses. McCall was tracked down, in Wyoming Territory, and tried, for the second time in Yankton, Dakota Territory, where he was convicted and hung.

Wild Bill's murder was news. Calamity Jane seized the opportunity to dramatically embellish what was actually a passing acquittance into a full-blown love affair with the gunfighter. Her fanciful tales of cradling the dying Hickock in her arms, and even tracking down the coward McCall, made their way into Eastern newspapers, and dime novels. Calamity left Deadwood in 1877 and continued to lead an unconventional, adventurous life, even performing in Buffalo Bill's Wild West show. She died at age 52, of complications from alcoholism in 1903, and was granted her dying wish of being buried next to Wild Bill Hickok.

Jack McCall (National Archives)

Deadwood's Leading Citizens

Among the fortune seekers flocking to Deadwood were some of the most iconic figures of the Old West, including Wyatt and Morgan Earp, and Doc Holliday. They did not stay long enough the make their mark, but some less familiar personalities did stay long enough to make a lasting impression on Deadwood, and the history of the West.

Colorado Charlie Utter headed the wagon train that brought Wild Bill, Calamity Jane, and a whole lot of prostitutes into Deadwood. The former trapper was fiercely loyal to, and protective of Wild Bill, and arranged and paid for the funeral. Upon arrival, while his buddy gravitated to the saloons, Colorado Charlie established a Pony Express type operation, delivering mail

Colorado Charlie at Wild Bill's grave. (National Archives)

between Deadwood, and Fort Laramie in Wyoming Territory.

He also opened up a couple of dance halls, but ultimately, they burned down. By 1880, Colorado Charlie moved on to New Mexico, and then Texas, where he opened some gambling halls. In 1888, he moved to Panama, where he opened a pharmacy, and practiced medicine. The circumstances surrounding his death are unknown.

Arriving in Deadwood the day before Hickok's slaying, was a man who would be instrumental in the civilizing of Deadwood: Seth Bullock. Along with his friend and partner Sol Star, they opened a hardware store, but the charismatic Bullock quickly established himself as a man who could peacefully resolve disputes among the rambunctious miners. In 1877, he became Deadwood's first sheriff and would go on to become a senator in Montana Territory. Among his contributions to Deadwood was the establishment of a Board of Health, as well as the town's first cemetery. He became a confidant to Teddy Roosevelt and served with the Black Hills

Seth Bullock (National Archives)

Rough Riders during the Spanish-American War. He died in 1919 at the age of seventy at his beloved Bullock Hotel.

Sol Star and Seth Bullock were business partners and lifelong friends. In addition to the Hardware store, the duo become heavily involved in agriculture, cattle ranching, and milling grain. Star was Deadwood's mayor from 1877 until his death in 1917.

It has been estimated that, in the early days of Deadwood, 90% of the women were 'sporting girls', the most famous of which was Dora DuFran, an English immigrant, who started prying her trade in Deadwood when she was fifteen. She worked her way up to owning her own brothel and gained a reputation for being kind to her employees, including Calamity Jane. She had an entrepreneurial streak and opened

Sol Starr (National Archives)

several brothels in the Black Hills, and is credited with coining the term 'cathouse' because of her fondness for felines. She lived until 1939.

WHAT HAPPENED NEXT?

On September 26, 1879, the bane of frontier towns, fire, swept through the center of Deadwood, destroying over three hundred buildings, and leaving a couple of thousand inhabitants homeless. At about 2:00 am, a busy baker had knocked over an oil lamp, and the fire quickly jumped to the nearby wooden structures. The blaze raged through downtown, razing such noteworthy structures as the courthouse (with all its records), Al Swearengen's recently remodeled Gem Variety Theater, and, regrettably, Nuttal & Mann's Saloon No. 10, the site of Wild Bill's untimely demise. The resourceful population immediately started to rebuild, and within six months, most of Deadwood was back in business, although many residents left town, never to return.

By 1890, the population had been cut in half, to about 2300, despite the arrival of the Fremont, Elkhorn, and Missouri Valley Railroad. Again, devastating fires engulfed Deadwood in 1894, and 1899, the latter closing the Gem Theater for the final time. By the 1920s the gold rush was long over, and Deadwood's population dropped to about 2500. In 1929, a four-foot-tall inch leftover prospector, calling himself Potato Creek Johnny, found one of the world's largest gold nuggets, weighing in at 7¾ troy ounces. The colorful old miner, was a local Deadwood celebrity, until his death in 1943. Fires continued to ravage what was left of the town, including an out-of-control forest fire in 1959, which destroyed over sixty structures.

Through the decades, however, Deadwood maintained its Wild West personality, with gambling legally surviving until 1947, and the last brothels remaining until 1980 (the good ole days are gone forever). Although Deadwood was named a National Historic Landmark in 1961, the town's fortunes didn't begin to rise until 1989, thanks to the legalization of gambling. Today, the former miners' camp is a legitimate tourist destination, hosting three-dozen casinos, three thousand and five hundred slot machines and over a hundred card tables.

WHAT DO I DO WHEN I GET THERE?

Deadwood Today

There is plenty to do; Main Street is a long line of saloons, casinos, and Old West-themed shops and boutiques. The Visitor Center, which provides maps and coupon books is located downtown on Siever Street, and a free trolley stops at all hotels and motels, as well as key locations in town. Some must-dos are as follows.

Adams Museum, 54 Sherman St., Deadwood, South Dakota, (605)578-1714

The Black Hills' oldest history museum has some unique treasures, including a prehistoric plesiosaur (marine reptile). The real draw, however, are the artifacts associated with Deadwood's most famous inhabitants, including Wild Bill's 1860 Army Colt revolver, and Potato Creek Johnny's original 7.3-ounce gold nugget.

Days of '76 Museum, 18 Seventy-Six Drive, Deadwood, South Dakota, (605)578-1657

Mt. Moriah Cemetery

Located on the north end of town next to the rodeo grounds, near the stream where gold was first discovered in Deadwood Gulch, the first-class museum showcases relics associated with the town's first settlers in 1876 including Calamity Jane's Winchester rifle, and Buffalo Bill's gauntlets. Displays also chronicle Deadwood's Days of 76, an annual five-day celebration in July, of the town's history featuring parades and rodeo events.

Mt. Moriah Cemetery, Mt. Moriah Dr., Deadwood, South Dakota, (605)722-0837

Although only several blocks from downtown, it's a steep uphill trek, so you need to go by car or a tour bus. There is a small Visitor Center that offers maps for a self-guided tour. The cemetery providing the final resting place of such Western notables as Wild Bill Hickock, Calamity Jane, Seth Bullock, and Deadwood's most famous madam, Dora Dufran, was established in 1876. Wild Bill was originally interred at the Boot Hill cemetery, which was down the hill from Mt. Moriah, but moved to the present burial site in 1879. The original wooden marker over his grave, composed and erected by his friend, read:

Wild Bill, J. B. Hickock killed by the assassin Jack McCall in Deadwood, Black Hills, August 2, 1876. Pard, we will meet again in the happy hunting ground to part no more. Goodbye. Colorado Charlie, C. H. Utter.

Several monuments on the gravesite have been chipped away by souvenir hunters through the decades, and the present sculpture is enclosed by a fence. Lying in eternal peace beside the famed pistoler is none other than Martha 'Calamity Jane' Canary, who was granted her dying to wish to be buried beside her fantasy lover.

Broken Boot Gold Mine, Upper Main Street, Deadwood, South Dakota, (605)578-9997

About a mile south of downtown, underground mine tours are given every thirty minutes, and kids, of all ages, can pan for gold.

IS THERE ANYTHING ELSE?

LEAD (pronounce Leed), SOUTH DAKOTA:

Located a few miles west of Deadwood, the old mining town was closely associated with Deadwood during the mining heyday of the late nineteenth century. It was near Lead where, in 1876, the Homestake Mine was established over a small part of the most significant gold vein in American history, which would go on to produce 10% of the world's gold supply for the next one hundred and twenty-five years, remaining open until 2002. Lead doesn't have the star power of its more famous neighbor, but it does have the Black Hills Mining Museum (325 W. Main St., Lead, South Dakota), which displays artifacts and photographs tied to the region's gold mining history. Today, only one gold mine remains in operation in the Black Hills.

Mount Rushmore National Memorial, 13000Hwy. 244, Keystone, SD 57751, (605)574-2523 (mtrushmorenationalmemorial.com)

Only about fifty miles from Deadwood is the national treasure of Mt. Rushmore. Carved into the Black Hills are the faces of the four presidents that guided the young nation through its first one hundred and twenty-five years: George Washington, Thomas Jefferson, Theodore Roosevelt, and Abraham Lincoln. Appropriately, the four chief executives all shared a bond of having strong ties to the West. Washington, as a

Mt. Rushmore

young surveyor, immediately grasped the unlimited potential of the then-Western frontier. Throughout his life, he would speculate in land transactions in the western fringes of the infant nation. At the time of his death, in 1799, he owned over 50,000 acres in the western portions of Virginia, Pennsylvania, Kentucky, and the Ohio country. Thomas Jefferson, early on, realized that for the United States to prosper, it must stretch from sea to shining sea, and was the driving force behind the Lewis and Clark expedition. Abraham Lincoln, although overwhelmed with the Civil War, never lost sight of the vast potential of the Western Territories. In 1862, he shepherded through Congress the Homestead Act, which opened millions of acres in the West to settlement and cultivation, and the Pacific Railway Act, which created the great transcontinental railroad. Teddy Roosevelt, the pampered dude from New York, underwent a powerful physical and mental transformation and began a lifelong fascination with the West when he fled to Dakota Territory to overcome the grief from losing both his wife and his mother, within hours of each other on Valentine's Day, 1884.

It took sculptor Gutzon Borglum and a crew of four hundred workers fourteen years to complete the four-hundred-and-sixty-five-foot-tall masterpiece. The Borglum View Terrace provides an excellent photo opportunity, and there is a half-mile walking trail that leads you a little closer to the sculpture. The Sculptor's Studio gives you a glimpse of Borglum's daily routine, during construction. Nightly, during the summer, there is a spectacular Evening Lighting Ceremony.

Crazy Horse Memorial, SD Hwy. 16, between Hill City and Custer (605)673-4681 (crazyhorsememorial.org)

Crazy Horse Memorial

About fifty miles from Deadwood, and fifteen miles from Mt. Rushmore, work is underway on a mountain rock carving of legendary Lakota Sioux warrior Crazy Horse. The proposed sculpture dwarfs Mt. Rushmore, and it has been under construction since 1948. Yes, you read that correctly. The ambitious project has been in the works for over seventy years and is nowhere close to completion. The catalyst behind the six hundred and forty-one feet long, and five hundred and sixty-three feet tall memorial was Korczak Ziolkowski, who worked on Mt. Rushmore. Since his death in 1982, his family has taken over the reins of the seemingly unfinishable monumental carving, supervising about fifteen daily workers. The Crazy Horse Memorial Visitor Complex encompasses a Native American Educational and Cultural Center and the Indian Museum of North America. The museum displays some intriguing artifacts, including a couple of knives owned by Crazy Horse.

WHERE CAN I WET MY WHISTLE?

Old Style Saloon No. 10, 657 Main Street, Deadwood, South Dakota, (800)952-9398 (saloon10.com)

Old Style Saloon No. 10

Although not the original location of the infamous killing, it is a fun, rowdy place, with plenty of Old West atmosphere. Its walls are filled with thousands of photographs, and artifacts, including Wild Bill's 'death chair', which miraculously survived the periodic fires. In the summer the 'Shooting of Wild Bill' is reenacted four times daily.

Wild Bill Bar & Trading Post, 624 Main Street, Deadwood, South Dakota, (605)430-0889

Located on the actual location of Nuttal and Mann's No. 10 Saloon, which burned down in the fire of 1879. For $5 you can wander downstairs to the basement and take a self-guided tour of the lower level, where Jack McCall did his notorious slaying. In 1876, the basement level was actually at street level, and strategically placed is a blood-stained table, complete with a spilled glass of whiskey, and the scattered dead man's hand. Of course, all of the

Wild Bill's Bar and Trading Post

furnishings are replicas, but it's still pretty cool, and worth five bucks (and you can bring your beer).

WHAT ABOUT GRUB?

Deadwood Social Club, 557 Main Street, Deadwood, South Dakota

Located upstairs from the Old Style Saloon No. 10, has great steaks, and Italian dishes. Stick with the steak.

Legends Steakhouse, 709 Main Street, Deadwood, South Dakota, (800)584-7005 (silveradofranklin.com)

Located in the Silverado Hotel and Gaming Complex, its superb steaks have been enjoyed by a variety of celebrities, including John Wayne, and Babe Ruth. (In 1922, the Bambino was in town to play an exhibition barn-storming game, for which he was suspended for six weeks of the 1923 season since such games were illegal for players that had played in the World Series).

WHERE CAN I PUT MY BOOTS UNDER A BED?

Bullock Hotel

Historic Bullock Hotel, 633 Main Street, Deadwood, South Dakota, (605)578-1745 (historicbullock.com)

The town's first hotel built in 1895 on the site of Seth Bullock's store, which burned down in the 1894 fire. Bullock spent an astonishing $40,000 to build the Bullock Hotel, a luxurious Bullock Hotel three-story brick structure, complete with indoor plumbing. The hotel went through a major renovation in 1990 but retains the Old West ambiance (and the indoor plumbing). The hotel's restaurant, 'Bully', was named after Bullock's unlikely pal, Teddy Roosevelt. It goes without saying that the hotel is haunted by the dead owner, and there are nightly ghost tours.

The Lodge at Deadwood, 100 Pine Crest Lane, Deadwood, South Dakota, (877)393-5634 (deadwoodlodge.com)

It's a little over a mile from downtown, but it is a stop on the downtown trolley. Although you're not in the middle of the action, the hotel offers spectacular views of the Black Hills and is a little more upscale than the downtown hotels.

WHAT SHOULD I WATCH AND READ BEFORE I HIT THE TRAIL?

BOOKS

- *Deadwood: The Golden Years* (1981, by Wilson Parker)—a thorough history of Deadwood, with an emphasis on 1875–1925

- *Wild Bill: The True Story of the American Frontier's First Gunfighter* (2019, by Tom Clavin)—*New York Times* bestselling author explores the almost mythical life of the West's most famous gunfighter.

VIDEOS

- *Deadwood* (HBO, three seasons, 2004–2006)—The critically acclaimed and award-winning drama only lasted three seasons but was followed by a movie in 2019, which tied up some loose ends. Despite the historically realistic-looking set, and the fantastic acting, Old West enthusiasts initially panned the series. Why? The language. To be fair, the language is bad. Real bad. And non-stop. Eventually, the traditional Old West enthusiasts got over it. Why? The series is good. Real good. Great sets, and historical characters, such as Calamity Jane, Wild Bill Hickok (albeit short-lived), Seth Bullock, and Al Swearengen make this a must-see for any Western fan (see p. 112).
- *Deadwood: The Movie* (2019, HBO)—thirteen years after the series ended, the film picks up ten years later in 1889 and doesn't miss a beat.
- *Wild Bill* (1995, MGM)—Jeff Bridges as Wild Bill and Ellen Barkin as Calamity Jane in this highly fictionized account of the gunfighter's last days.

TIPS FROM THE TRAIL

Spend at least a couple of days in Deadwood to take advantage of the Old West-style nightlife. Just beware that the Sturgis, South Dakota Motorcycle Rally usually takes place the first week in August, attracting over a half-million bikers to the Black Hills. Consequently, Deadwood's PG-rated entertainment goes up a notch.

The Real Al Swearingen and the Gem Theater

Gem Theater

For Western buffs, the allure of the HBO 'Deadwood' series is that it is based on real early inhabitants of the boomtown. A central figure of the series is Al Swearengen, played by Ian McShane, who rules his Gem Theater, and its soiled doves, with a firm, and violent hand. The real Ellis Albert Swearingen was born in 1845 in Iowa and arrived in Deadwood in May 1876, establishing the Cricket Saloon, on the muddy Main Street. The following year he opened up the Gem Theater, which also served as a gambling hall, saloon, dance hall, and brothel. Along with gambling, sex, and alcohol, the Gem provided varied top-notch entertainment, including dancers, singers, comedians, and even trapeze artists. The entertainment mecca was not without its seedy underbelly. Many of the young women in Swearingen's employ, were not only underage but had been violently forced into the oldest profession. Drug addiction, disease, and even suicides were occupational hazards for working girls. Swearengen's personal life was what you would imagine it would be. All three of his marriages would end amid allegations of spousal abuse.

The wildly profitable Gem burned down in the devastating fire of September 1879, but Swearengen immediately, and quickly rebuilt. The result was an elaborate, modern structure, including a large saloon area, with gaming tables, surrounded by nineteen private boxes hanging from the second floor. The New Gem housed a theater, around which hung private boxes, allowing for more sensual pursuits. Spectacular entertainment was provided, including the scandalous Parisian 'cancan' dance. Into the 1890s, the Gem continued to prosper, until finally shutting its doors in 1897. It remained closed for two years, reopened in 1899, but burned down shortly thereafter. The inhabitants of a now more respectable Deadwood were glad to see it go. It was never rebuilt. Its original location is now a parking lot, next to the Celebrity Hotel, on Lower Main Street.

Swearingen left town, and not much more is known about him, other than, on November 15, 1904, his body was found between trolley tracks in Denver, Colorado. It was determined that he died of a blunt force to the head, but it is not known if, he simply fell from a trolley, or was murdered.

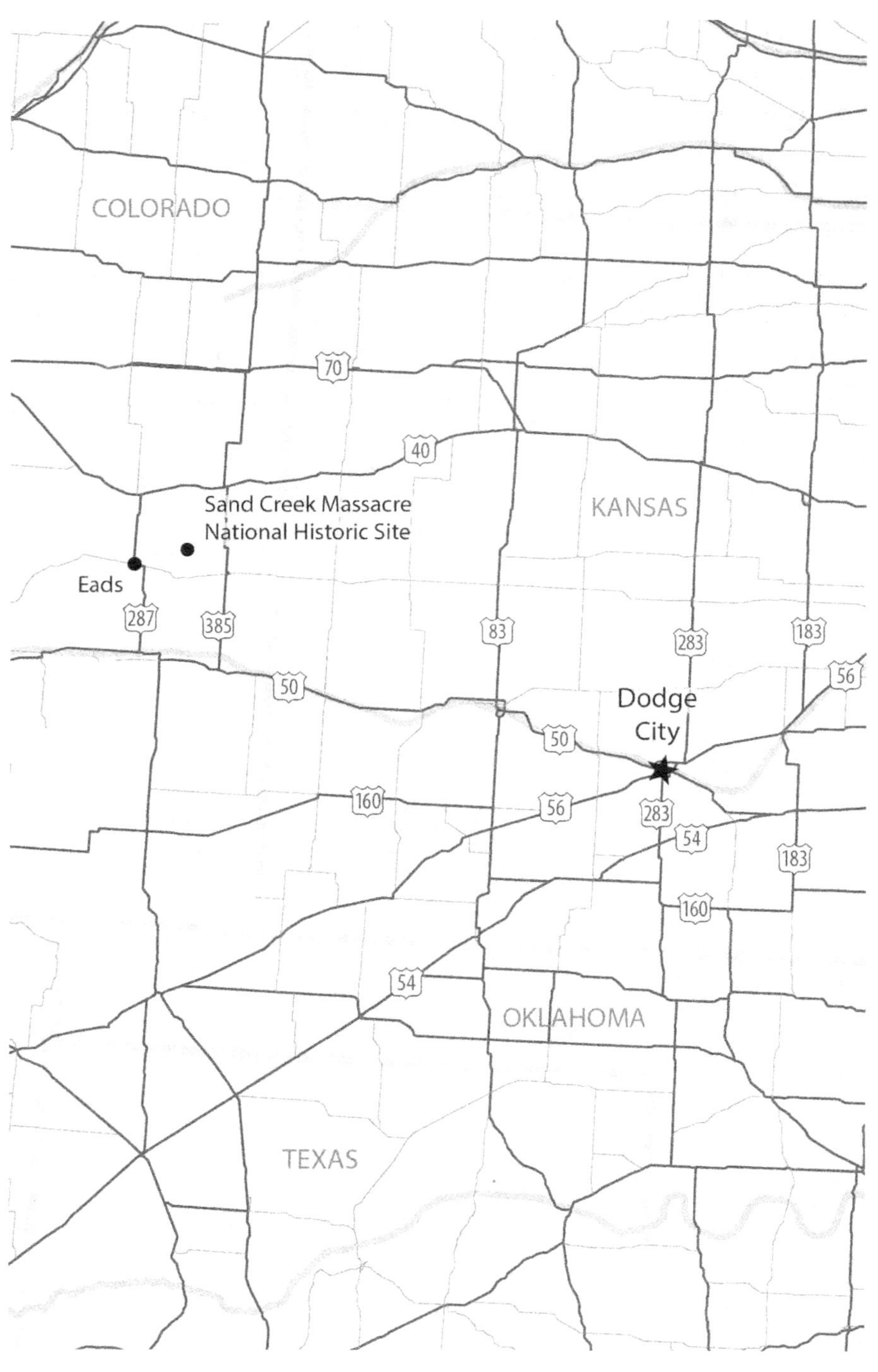

COLORADO
KANSAS
OKLAHOMA
TEXAS
Sand Creek Massacre
National Historic Site
Eads
Dodge
City
70
40
287
385
83
283
183
56
50
50
160
56
283
54
183
160
54

Dodge City

Kansas

Dodge City in the 1870s (Courtesy of Kansas State Historical Society)

WHAT HAPPENED HERE?

When one thinks of an Old West town, Dodge City, Kansas, immediately comes to mind. It is fondly remembered as a wild and woolly Cowtown that attracted not only cowboys, but gamblers, buffalo hunters, prostitutes, outlaws, and, of course, lawmen. Oh yeah, and saloon keepers. In the 1870s, the Town had sixteen saloons for a thousand residents. Dodge City's raucous reputation survives today. Most are familiar with the phrase, 'get out of Dodge', slang for expeditiously extricating oneself from an unpleasant scenario. Dodge City got a boost in familiarity in 1955 when the TV series 'Gunsmoke', set in Dodge City, ruled the airways for twenty years. Although Marshal Dillon, Doc, Miss Kitty, Chester, and later, the simple-minded, but lovable Festus were fictional characters, Dodge City was as real as it gets.

Geographically, Dodge City is situated on the 100th Meridian, the imaginary longitudinal line that runs north and south, through North Dakota, South Dakota, Nebraska, Kansas, Oklahoma, and Texas, considered the natural boundary between East and West. To the west of this invisible line begins the Great American Desert or the Great Plains, once home to millions of Buffalo, and the Plains Indians who depended on them for food, shelter, and life itself.

Dodge City's origins on the barren west Kansas plains emanated from Fort Dodge, located about five miles to the west of the future cow town. Fort Dodge was constructed in 1865, on the north bank of the Arkansas River, to protect the thousands of settlers venturing west on the Santa Fe Trail, the famous commercial route utilized by thousands of wagons between Franklin, Missouri, and Santa Fe, New Mexico. The Fort served as a base of operations for combating the thousands of Comanche, Apache, and Kiowa Indians who lived on the Kansas plains. The most famous army officers of the era, including William Sherman, Phil Sheridan, Winfield Hancock, and George Armstong Custer would pass through its gates.

What started out as a couple of sod structures five miles from the Fort, where troopers could imbibe in some whiskey, without being under the watchful eyes of the officers, rapidly developed into a commercial gathering spot for not only the soldiers, but for travelers, traders, and buffalo hunters. The Kansas plains were rich with the American bison, and, it has been estimated that, ultimately, over one and a half million buffalo hides would be shipped back east from Dodge. In fact, initially, the settlement was named Buffalo City until it was realized that there was already a town with that moniker, so it was eventually changed to Dodge City.

A Pile of Buffalo Skins Being Shipped from Dodge City
(University of Michigan Library)

In September 1872, the Atchison, Topeka, and Santa Fe Railroad reached Buffalo City, attracting even more buffalo hunters, including future Western icons Col. William F. 'Buffalo Bill' Cody, Bat and Ed Masterson, and Wyatt Earp, who would return to Dodge years later in much more celebrated roles. The railroad not only helped the already lucrative buffalo trade but made Dodge City a destination for Texas cattle.

Since the end of the Civil War, large herds consisting of thousands of Texas Longhorn cattle had been driven up from Texas to the railheads in Kansas for transport to the beef-hungry markets in the East. Along with the Longhorn cattle, however, came a tick-borne disease, known as 'Texas fever', which proved deadly to non-Texas cattle. To protect home-grown livestock, the Kansas legislature drew an imaginary quarantine 'line', running north-south which banned the Texas cattle from anywhere east of the line separating the more populous eastern part of the state from the sparsely populated western section. Consequently, towns in mid-Kansas, such as Abilene, Wichita, and Ellsworth prospered.

Of course, along with the good, came the bad. The towns were notoriously violent and rowdy. Steady lawmen, men with the grit and composure to control large numbers of alcohol-fueled cowboys, justifiably blowing off some steam, following a couple of months on the trail, were a necessity to prevent total lawlessness.

In 1876, the Kansas legislature moved the quarantine line further west, thereby eliminating Abilene, Ellsworth, and Wichita as cattle drive destinations, and leaving Dodge City, on the western edge of Kansas, as the sole remaining major railhead along the Santa Fe Trail. Dodge City was about to start its decade-long reign as the Cowboy Capital, in which over five million head of Texas Longhorns would pass through 'the wickedest town in America'.

With the moving of the quarantine line in 1876, Dodge City officials were well aware that a strong and competent law enforcement staff was required to keep some semblance of order, while still reaping the commercial benefits of catering to the free-spending thirsty cowboys. The mayor turned to a man who had been building a reputation as a cool, seemingly fearless, no-nonsense lawman in Wichita: Wyatt Earp. Or so the legend goes. The murky facts suggest that Earp's reappointment to the Wichita police force was in question since he had just been fined for beating up a candidate for city marshal, whose politics did not align with the Earp brothers. In any event, while in Wichita, Earp had perfected the art of 'buffaloing': the lightning-fast whacking of a troublesome cowpoke on the forehead with the barrel of a pistol, before the unsuspecting, and probably inebriated drover knew what hit him.

In May 1876, Earp ventured to Dodge City, where he was appointed deputy Marshal, and reunited with an old friend from his Buffalo hunting days, William Barclay 'Bat' Masterson. Despite only being twenty-two years old, Masterson was already well known on the Kansas plains as a tough customer. In 1874, he and a couple of dozen buffalo hunters, trapped in a Texas-panhandle trading post, held off hundreds of Cheyenne, Comanche, and Kiowa warriors in what came to be known as the Second Battle of Adobe Walls. When Wyatt arrived in Dodge, Bat was recovering from a leg wound he had received in a fracas he had gotten into with an Army corporeal over a saloon girl in Sweetwater, Texas, that had left both the soldier and unfortunate saloon girl dead. Bat's limp didn't stop Wyatt from securing him a position as a deputy, and Bat would become a familiar site walking the streets of Dodge, carrying a cane, and donning a derby hat.

The Earps and Mastersons were clannish breeds. Wyatt had bought along his third wife, Mattie, and met up with his brother, James, who was already in town, running a brothel, and they were soon joined by their brother Morgan. Ed and Jim Masterson followed their charismatic sibling to the wickedest town in the West.

Bat Masterson and Wyatt Earp in Their 20s (Denver Public Library)

Earp and Masterson promptly established a 'deadline', prohibiting the carrying of firearms north of the railroad tracks, the locale of respectable establishments on Front Street. South of the 'deadline' was a wide-open array of saloons, dancehalls, and brothels. Lots of brothels. In fact, western lore holds that the term 'red light district' originated in Dodge City. Railroad men would take red caboose lanterns with them, when they visited the town's houses of ill repute, and leave the red lantern outside the door while they were inside, taking care of business.

The effectiveness of the lawmen of Dodge caught the attention of Edward Zane Judson, a prolific author of dime novels, better known as Ned Buntline. Buntline had been instrumental in thrusting Buffalo Bill Cody into the national limelight, and would never let facts get in the way of a compelling tale. The colorful author would later claim that it in 1876 he traveled to Dodge City to present a special gift to Dodge City's famous lawmen for 'the color they supplied' in keeping the peace. Buntline maintained that that after viewing the Colt Manufacturing Company's exhibit of long-barreled revolvers at the Philadelphia Exposition, he specially ordered five.45 caliber pistol with an elongated eighteen-inch barrel, with 'Ned' deeply carved into the walnut handle.

Buntline ceremoniously presented the 'Buntline Specials' to Dodge City's finest: Bat Masterson, Wyatt Earp, Luke Short, Bill Tilghman, Charlie Basset, and Neil Brown. Historians have since cast serious doubt on the existence of the 'Buntline Specials', but nonetheless, the myth of the long-barreled pistol is firmly ingrained in Western lore, and specifically associated with Wyatt Earp. The former lawman, in his later years, would rave about the 'Buntline Special', calling it his favorite sidearm. The elongated eighteen inch barrel was perfect for 'buffaloing'.

The West's most famous and infamous characters passed through Dodge City. In addition to Bat Masterson, and Wyatt Earp, Wild Bill Hickok, John Wesley Hardin, Jesse James, and John Henry 'Doc' Holliday all spent some time in the Gomorrah of the Plains. Doc, accompanied by his own again off again paramour, 'Big Nose Kate' Elder, would even practice dentistry when he could be pried away from the gambling tables at the Long Branch. The volatile Holliday was an unlikely, yet loyal friend to Earp, who would occasionally deputize the sometimes-sober gambler when the need arose.

Front Street in 1874 (Ford County Historical Society, Dodge City, KS)

In 1877, Bat was elected Sheriff of Ford County, Kansas, and arranged a position as Dodge City marshal for his older brother, Ed, which would have disastrous results. Ed was a capable lawman but did not have the rough edge of his younger brother. Ed's trusting nature may have contributed to his demise on the evening of April 9, 1878. That night, outside the Lady Gay Saloon, the Marshall was confronted by an armed drunken cowboy. Although Ed had disarmed the man, earlier, the trusting lawman had simply returned the weapon to the drover's trail boss. Ed was killed instantly from a blast at point-blank range. Bat raced to the scene, gunfire ensued, and Ed's assailant soon lay dead on the streets of Dodge.

In October 1878, Bat Masterson would put together, possibly, the most famous posse of the Old West, to track down the killer of the hugely popular Dodge City entertainer, Dora Hand. The attractive Hand, known in the saloons of Dodge, by her stage name, Fannie Keenan, was shot and killed on that fall night, as she lay sleeping in a house owned by the married mayor of Dodge City, Ed 'Dog' Kelly, who was luckily away. The slayer, James 'Spike' Kenedy, had perceived the mayor as a rival for the affections of the voluptuous showgirl and fired two shots into the frame structure. One bullet passed through the nightgown of another entertainer, Fannie Garrettson, who was in Kelly's bed, and the second shot ripped through a partition, instantly killing Dora.

Bat Masterson, Wyatt Earp, Charlie Basset, and Bill Tilghman rode a hundred miles, braving a snowstorm, before catching up with Kenedy, before he could reach his father's Texas ranch. Bat shot Kenedy in the shoulder; Wyatt killed his horse; and Kenedy was brought back to Dodge to stand trial for the murder of Dora Hand. Kenedy's father, a wealthy Texas rancher, traveled to Dodge, to make sure justice was served. It was. His son was acquitted, and it was rumored that Dodge City officials were $25,000.00 richer. The funeral for Dora Hand was the largest Dodge City would ever witness.

In 1879, Bat Masterson was also appointed Deputy US Marshal. Despite wearing two different law enforcement hats, Bat managed to spend a considerable amount of time gambling and also had an ownership interest in the Lone Star and Dance Hall Saloon. The busy Masterson lost his bid for reelection for Ford County Sheriff. The political tide was beginning to turn against the hard-nosed tactics of Earp and Masterson, and later on that year, the two lawmen would go their separate ways, but remain lifelong friends.

In April of 1881, Bat would be gambling in the boomtown of Tombstone, when he would receive word that his brother Ed was having difficulties in Dodge, and needed assistance. Without hesitation, he began his eleven hundred-mile trek to Dodge. As soon as Bat stepped off the train in Dodge, a gun battle ensued on Front Street, leaving his brother's antagonist dead. Bat was promptly arrested, and he pled guilty to discharging a pistol, was fined $8, and promptly got out of Dodge on the next train.

Bat would return to Dodge again in the Spring of 1883 when he and Wyatt heeded the call of Luke Short, their old friend from the earlier, wilder days in Dodge. Short was now the owner of the Long Branch Saloon but was being forced out of business by the new reform-minded powers that be in Dodge. Short sent telegrams to his former law enforcement compadres, including Earp, Doc Holliday, and Masterson, to help set things straight. When word got out that Short's friends, including the two most famous men to have had ever worn a badge, had been summoned, bloodshed was anticipated.

Dodge awaited the arrival of the former lawmen, and what had been dubbed the 'Dodge City War'. The anxious onlookers were disappointed. The Dodge City War ended without a shot being fired, and Luke Short was back in business at the Long Branch. The reformers were not prepared to face down Earp, Masterson, and what had been dubbed the Dodge City Peace Commission.

The two lawmen would live into the twentieth century and witness the end of the frontier. Bat would spend his last years as a New York City sportswriter (p. 131), and Wyatt would retire to Southern California, where he would unsuccessfully attempt to peddle his life story to an emerging Hollywood. Bat would later write that Wyatt was 'absolutely destitute of physical fear... a loyal friend and equally dangerous enemy'. Although Wyatt's defining moment in Western lore would occur, not in Dodge, but outside a corral in Tombstone, Arizona, his teaming with Masterson in Dodge City, would come to be viewed as the pinnacle of frontier justice.

Dodge City Peace Commission
(National Archives)

Bat and Wyatt would continue to be the subject of numerous books, movies, and television shows for the next hundred years. Western shows dominated the movie and television screens of the 1950s and 1960s. Three of the most popular television series emanate from the glory days of Dodge City: 'Gunsmoke', in which a fictional composite character, Marshal Matt Dillion, kept the peace in Dodge City for a record twenty seasons; 'Bat Masterson' featuring Gene Barry in the title role, as a dapper cane-carrying ex-lawman subduing evil-doers throughout the West; and The Life and Legend of Wyatt Earp, in which Hugh O'Brien conspicuously totes an eighteen-inch 'Buntline Special'.

WHAT HAPPENED NEXT?

In March 1885, the Quarantine line moved further west to the Kansas-Colorado border, thus eliminating the Texas cattle drives, and later on that same year, two devastating fires destroyed most of the buildings on Front Street. Dodge City officials also began enforcing the statewide alcohol prohibition. (Kansas would remain a 'dry state' until 1948). Putting a nail in the coffin of Dodge City's heydays were two crippling blizzards in January 1886, which wiped out as much as 80% of the home-grown cattle.

El Capitan – commemorating the Texas Longhorn vital role in the history of Dodge City.

When the cattle drives ceased, the environs around Dodge City turned to farming. The rich soil of the Kansas plains was well suited to grow wheat, and Dodge City became a center for farmers and homesteaders.

A replica Front Street was reconstructed in the 1950s, northwest of its original locale, in an area adjoining the old Boot Hill graveyard. The exteriors of the buildings were authentically duplicated utilizing photographs from the 1880s.

The cast of "Gunsmoke."

The tourist trade was brisk in the mid-1950s into the 1960s, thanks in large measure to the popularity of 'Gunsmoke' cast members, including James Arness would occasionally visit the real Dodge City, to much fanfare. Dodge still periodically hosts 'Gunsmoke reunions', and in 2017 a life-sized statue of James Arness as Matt Dillion was unveiled on the Dodge City Trail of Fame.

In 1970, as part of an urban renewal project, to widen Front Street, and provide off-street parking, the brick Victorian buildings that had replaced the wooden structures on Front Street were demolished. Sadly, where the main commercial section once thrived on Front Street between 1st and 2nd Streets is now a parking lot.

Finally, in 1989, Dodge's oldest building, the one-hundred-and-two-year-old Stiker and Bell Building simply collapsed. The only remaining structure from the Wyatt Earp and Bat Masterson days is the Mueller-Schmidt House, which was what was once Front Street. Built in 1881 out of limestone by German immigrants and

What was once Front Street.

is now a museum. Today, Dodge is a small city of about 30,000, and the main industry is meat packing.

WHAT DO I DO WHEN I GET THERE?

Historic Trolley Tours, 400 W. Wyatt Earp Blvd., Dodge City, Kansas, (620)225-8186

Hop on and off the trolley, with a narrated tour of the historic district, Fort Dodge, and the Santa Fe Trail Tracks.

Boot Hill Museum, 500 W. Wyatt Earp Blvd., Dodge City, KS 67801, (620)227-8188 (boothill.org)

Boot Hill Cemetery

The museum is located on the original burial ground for Dodge, which ceased taking new customers in 1879 when the land became too valuable.

Recreated headstones, telling about the original occupants of the old graveyard are scattered about the entrance to the People of the Plains Exhibit Building. The Native American gallery displays artifacts and photographs associated with the Plains Indians, the original occupants of the area. The collection includes Native American arrowheads, tools, moccasins, and even a peace pipe.

The remainder of the museum exhibits are displayed behind the reconstructed facade of Front Street, which adjoins the old Boot Hill property and is encompassed in the museum grounds. The history of Dodge City and the Old West is preserved through more than 60,000 artifacts, photographs, and documents displayed through themed galleries.

The Army and Railroad gallery exhibits items associated with the Army forts that protected travelers along the Santa Fe Trail, and the railroad that reached Dodge in 1872.

The Buffalo Hunters and American Bison gallery includes a multimedia presentation examining the importance of the American buffalo to the region that literally shakes the floor during a stampede.

Other galleries display artifacts associated with cowboys, cattle drives, and farmers. For the baby boomers, there is a compelling gallery displaying memorabilia associated with movies and TV shows featuring Dodge City, including, of course, 'Gunsmoke'. The Guns That Won The West Exhibit features over two hundred rare and antique firearms. Although I may be nit-picking, one irritating aspect of the museum is that many of the displayed artifacts don't include any explanation as to their pedigree. That being said, the museum does have some compelling items, such as Bat Masterson's Colt.45 pistol, and a replica 'Buntline Special'. The museum grounds also have some original nineteenth-century buildings, such as the Fort Dodge Jail, a blacksmith shop, and schoolhouse, that were moved from other locales. During the summer, there are gunfights on Front Street, and dinner shows at the Long Branch Saloon.

Dodge City Trail of Fame, Gunsmoke Street, Dodge City, KS 67801, (620)561-1925 (dodgecitytrailoffame.org)

A walking tour goes the Old Dodge City National Historic District, marked with bronze medallions and statues honoring famous past inhabitants, and the actors who portrayed them in film and TV. Some of the actors have left their autographs, and hand-prints in cement, near their medallion. There is also a great life-sized sculpture of Doc Holliday playing poker.

Doc Holiday in his natural element.

You can pick up a map at the Visitors Center.

Miller-Schmidt House Home of Stone, 112 E. Vine St., Dodge City, KS 67801, (620)227-6791 (kansashistory.us)

The oldest remaining structure in Dodge City is now a museum, which showcases household furnishings from the 1880s.

Boothill Casino and Resort, 4000 W. Comanche St., Dodge City, KS 67801, (877)906-0777 (boothillcasino.com)

Typical small casino, although it does have a Western-themed motif, and some neat pictures. Something to do at night in this sleepy town.

Gunfighters Wax Museum, 603 5th Ave., Dodge City, KS 67801, (316)225-7311 (teachershallfamedodgecityks.org)

Located in the upstairs of the Kansas Teachers Hall of Fame (I kid you not), this hokey, but fun museum is a throwback to the 1960s. Among the West's most famous wax dummies (Buffalo Bill, Jesse James, Billy the Kid, etc.), are scattered such diverse figures as Dracula and Presidents John F. Kennedy and Lyndon B. Johnson. If you're in town you might as well go.

Dodge City Feedlot Overlook, 11347 E. Wyatt Earp Blvd.

Located about two miles west of the main part of town, it is an overlook of… a cattle feedlot. As you read the storyboard explaining the history and importance of the cattle industry to Dodge, you can see (and smell), a few hundred head of cattle. Today meat processing is the main industry in Dodge, processing about 6000 cattle a day.

IS THERE ANYTHING ELSE?

Fort Dodge, Hwy 56/400

Five miles east of Dodge City is what is left of Fort Dodge, which was originally constructed in 1865, to protect settlers heading west on the Santa Fe Trail. Today it is the Kansas Veteran's Home, but some original structures remain, including the 'Custer House' the old officer's quarters which Custer may have stayed at, when he passed through Fort Dodge in 1868. The library on the grounds houses a small museum. The hours vary, depending on the season, and it's closed on Sundays.

Santa Fe Trail Tracks

Five miles east of Dodge City off Hwy 56, remnants of the Santa Fe Trail can be observed. With a little imagination, tourists can view large ruts in the weeds, evidencing the steady stream of wagons trudging along the Santa Fe Trail one hundred and fifty years ago.

Sand Creek Massacre National Historic Site, County Rd 54 & County Rd W, (near Eads), Colorado

Although a bit of a hike from Dodge City (about one hundred and eighty miles northwest of Dodge, along Highway 50), it is the site of one of the bloodiest atrocities in the history of the West. On November 29, 1864, about seven hundred federal soldiers, without provocation, attacked a village of approximately five hundred Cheyenne and Arapaho Indians. During the Civil War, Colorado was a vital source of gold for the cash-strapped Union. To protect the surge of new settlers, the Territorial Governor ordered that all Indian tribes relocate near military posts. Under the command of Col. John Chivington, the Colorado volunteers launched a surprise attack on the Indian village that left over one hundred and fifty dead; mostly women and children. If that wasn't bad enough, the following day the soldiers returned and grossly mutilated the cadavers. And if that wasn't bad enough, upon their triumph return to Denver, the soldiers were hailed as heroes and proudly displayed their grisly trophies of war, consisting of scalps, and other assorted body parts (use your imagination).

Although almost immediately recognized as a National disgrace, the Sand Creek battlefield, itself was ignored, and, over the ensuing decades became unrecognizable. Commencing in the 1980s, federal funds were secured, and efforts were undertaken to definitively locate the site, and properly recognize what occurred there. Descendants of Indian participants were intertied; aerial photographs were examined; and archaeological studies were undertaken until, finally in 2000, it was determined that the site of the village and battlefield encompassed over 12,000 acres not far from where Rush Creek meets Sand Creek, the site of today's National Historic Site.

The National Historic Site is definably 'no frills'; the Visitor Center is a double-wide trailer, and the visitor simply walks along a one-mile trail on a bluff overlooking the 'killing field'. Yet it is a moving, subdued experience that forces the visitor to recognize that, along with the astounding accomplishments achieved in the settlement of the West, there were also horrendous abuses, especially to the Indians.

The Long Branch Saloon, Boot Hill Museum

It's part of the Boot Hill Museum complex, so you have to pay the museum admission to get in, and so the hours are limited. You can get a beer, however, and some of the furnishings are reportedly from the original Long Branch saloon.

Long Branch Saloon

WHAT ABOUT GRUB?

Casey's Cowtown Club, 503 E. Trail, Dodge City, Kansas, (620)227-5225 (caseyscowtown.com)

Decent steak, with a Western decor. It's not Delmonico's, but it will have to do.

All in all, it's slim pickings (and I don't mean the lovable character actor). You can catch the dinner show at the Long Branch, or there is an Applebee's next to the Boot Hill Museum (what can I tell you?).

Long Branch today.

WHERE CAN I HANG MY HAT AND PUT MY BOOTS UNDER A BED?

Dodge House Hotel & Convention Center, 2408 W. Wyatt Earp Blvd., Dodge City, Kansas,
(620)225-9900(dodgehousehotelconventioncenter.com)

Serviceable, and it's close to the Mariah Hills Golf Course, and the Boot Hill Casino.

Boot Hill Bed & Breakfast, 603 Spruce Street, Dodge City, Kansas, (620)225-0111 (boothilldodgecity.com)

Located right by the Boot Hill Museum.

WHAT SHOULD I READ AND WATCH BEFORE I HIT THE TRAIL?

BOOKS

- *Dodge City: Wyatt Earp, Bat Masterson, and the Wickedest Town in the American West* (2016, by Tom Clavin)—a colorful and entertaining look at the cattle town in its prime, with a heavy emphasis on Earp and Masterson
- *Bat Masterson* (1979, by Robert DeArment)—the Masterson scholar painting a vivid portrait of this often-overlooked lawman
- *Dodge City and the Birth of the Wild West* (2017, by Robert R. Dykstra and Jo Ann Manfra)—highly researched look at the iconic cattle town and examination of whether its violent reputation is justified or exaggerated.

VIDEOS

- *Dodge City* (1939, Warner Home Video)—This early Western film stars the popular pairing of Errol Flynn and Olivia De Havilland. The film held its world premiere in Dodge City too much hoopla.
- *Gunsmoke* (Warner Home Video)—James Arness as Marshall Matt Dillion patrolled Dodge City for a record twenty TV seasons. To be honest, the earlier seasons are better. Toward the end of its run *Gunsmoke* fell into a predictable pattern in which at the beginning of the episode, Matt would have to leave town for some reason, leaving his deputy Festus (Ken Curtis) in charge. Things would promptly go array, but, with ten minutes left, Matt would ride into Town and straighten everything out. But it still beats anything on TV today.

Usually the last week in July through the first week of August, the Chamber of Commerce sponsors Dodge City Days (dodgecitydays.com), a ten-day celebration of the Western heritage of Dodge, featuring parades, rodeos, and, of course, shootouts; lots of shootouts. The highlight of the event features cowboys on horseback driving Longhorns down Wyatt Earp Boulevard!

It might seem that I've been a little harsh on Dodge City, but, admittedly, the whole experience is somewhat underwhelming. Particularly disappointing is that all the original structures are gone, and the recreated Front Street is not even in the footprint of the original. Where the iconic Long Branch Saloon once stood is now a parking lot. That being said, there is no disputing that, in Western Lore, Dodge City is fondly remembered as the last turbulent Cowtown of the frontier. The Boot Hill Museum does have some enthralling artifacts, the people working there are friendly and enthusiastic, and in 2016, *True West Magazine* named it the number 1 museum of the West! All in all, it is well worth a five-hour day trip from Kansas City or Denver.

BROADWAY BAT

Bat Masterson in His New York City Days (Library of Congress, LC-B21329-11)

After Masterson left Dodge, he continued to travel the boom towns of the west, seeking his elusive fortune, as a gambler, saloon entrepreneur, and, also occasionally wearing a badge. He and his wife, Emma ultimately landed in New York City in 1902, which they would call home for the rest of their lives.

Bat became a sportswriter for *Morning Telegraph*, which featured his biweekly column, 'Masterson's Views on Timely Topics'. Bat did not limit his topics to sports, and over the next eighteen years, Bat would entertain New Yorkers, with his prolific observations on almost any subject that crossed his mind. Making the lengthy articles readable, were Masterson's pithy comments, albeit confusing, such as, "There are more ways to kill a dog than by choking him to death with a piece of custard pie," and "Every dog, we are told has his day, unless there are more dogs than days."

Masterson's fame as a Western lawman and gunfighter preceded him to the Big Apple, and he relished his notoriety. He was a much sort after dinner guest, and easily mixed along the Great White Way with fellow writers, actors, athletes, and politicians, declaring that he was 'a Broadway guy'. Broadway playwright Damon Runyon even based his 'Sky Masterson' character in the smash hit 'Guys and Dolls', on the former lawman. Adding to Bat's high-profile social status was his appointment in 1905, as US Marshal for the Southern District of New York by Western enthusiast President Teddy Roosevelt.

On the morning of October 25, 1921, the old gunslinger was found slumped over his typewriter at the *Morning Telegraph*; dead of a massive heart attack, at sixty-eight. William Barclay 'Bat' Masterson had surely come a long way from being a buffalo hunter on the Kansas plains to being the toast of Broadway.

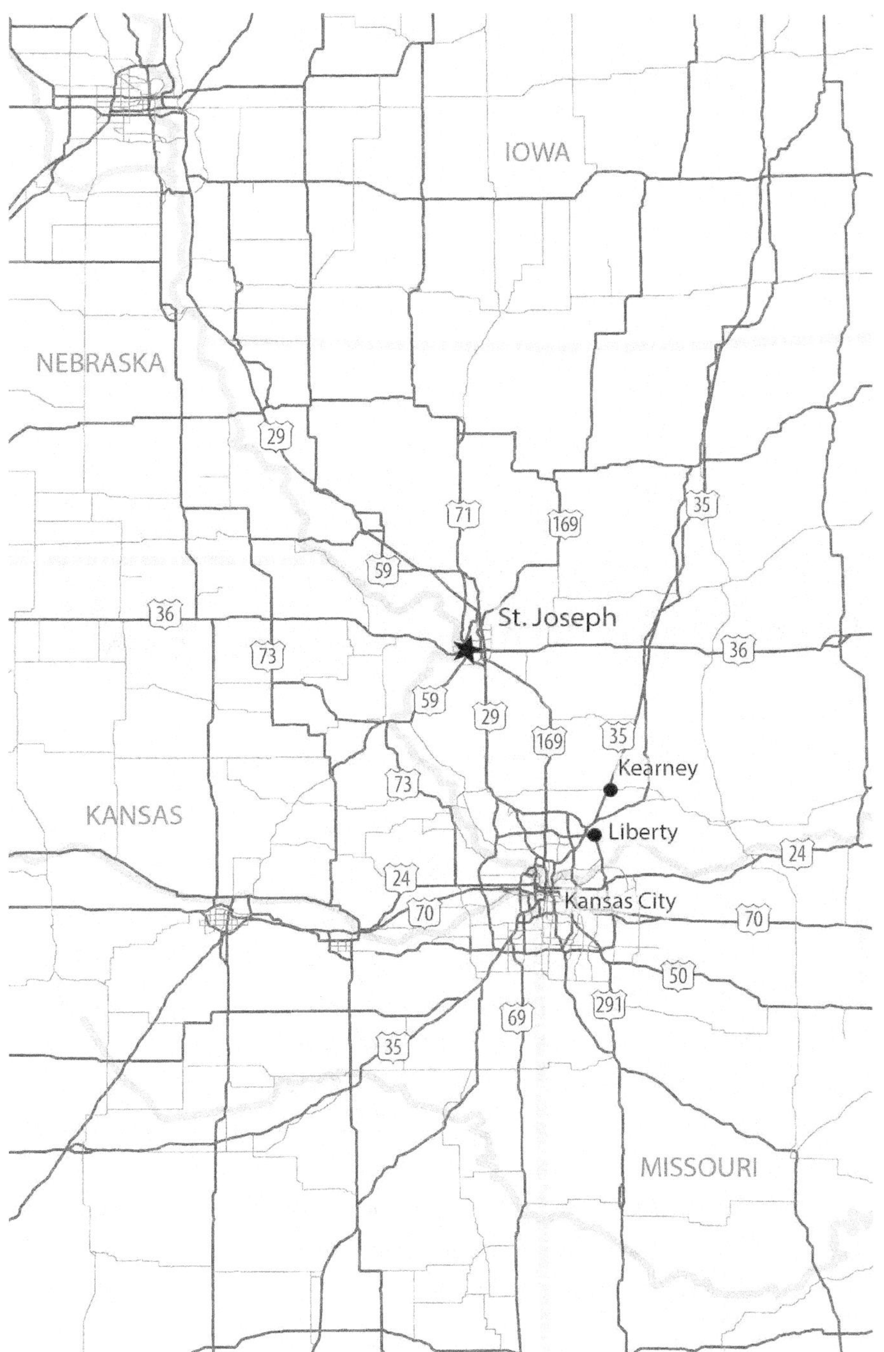

IOWA
NEBRASKA
29
71
169
35
59
36
73
36
St. Joseph
59
29
169
35
73
Kearney
KANSAS
Liberty
24
24
70
Kansas City
70
69
291
50
35
MISSOURI

St. Joseph

Missouri

St. Joseph (Depiction of the Modes of Transportation That Settled the West).

WHAT HAPPENED HERE?

Located on the banks of the Missouri River, and long considered a jumping-off point for those headed west to the Great American Desert and beyond, St. Joseph was the locale of not one but two legendary Old West events occurring exactly twenty-two years apart.

On April 3, 1860, America's first Pony Express rider took off from a stable in St. Joseph to ride the first leg of a 2,000-mile trek to deliver mail to Sacramento, California.

On April 3, 1882, the notorious outlaw Jesse James, while at home in St. Joseph, stood on a chair to dust a picture and was shot in the back of the head by fellow gang member Robert Ford.

The Pony Express

The Pony Express. It was the brainchild of three businessmen, each with a background in the freighting business: William Waddell, William Russell, and Alexander Majors. The three entrepreneurs formed Central Overland California and Pikes Peak Express Company and secured a lucrative government contract for quick mail delivery to booming California. The US government, on the brink of the Civil War, desired prompt communications to gold-rich California, and the Pony Express, using a relay system of solo riders, promised to deliver in ten days what took almost a month by stagecoach. Headquarters for the Pony Express was established on Penn Street in St. Joseph, at the Patee House, where the 2,000-mile trip's logistics were organized and implemented.

Along the route, one hundred and ninety way stations were established, four hundred station hands and two hundred riders were hired, and over five hundred horses were purchased. The horses, while not technically ponies, were smaller than most horses and could weigh no more than nine hundred pounds.

Because of the weight of the gear and the mail, riders could be no more than one hundred and twenty-five pounds, and an appetite for adventure proved a necessary attribute. The solicitation for riders reads: "WANTED: YOUNG, SKINNY, WIRY FELLOWS NOT OVER EIGHTEEN. MUST BE EXPERT PONY RIDERS WILLING TO RISK DEATH DAILY. ORPHANS PREFERRED."

Successful candidates were paid $25 per week, about five times the average salary at the time, and swore an oath to abstain from drinking alcohol, fighting, cursing, and abusing their horses. It was dangerous work, for sure. Each rider carried twenty pounds of mail in a leather saddle cover called a mochila. They rode approximately seventy-five miles on each leg of their relay, changing mounts every fifteen miles. The route went through what are now Missouri, Kansas, Nebraska, Colorado, Wyoming, Utah, Nevada, and California. The route ended in Sacramento, where the mail was forwarded by steamboat to San Francisco; a tremendous amount of work for one pouch of mail.

Among the obstacles on the perilous ten-day journey, were the daunting mountains of the Sierra Nevada, and Nevada's hostile Paiute Indian country. Incredibly, despite combating harsh terrain, extreme weather, and hostile Indians, only four riders died while delivering for the Pony Express. In fact, it was more hazardous to be a station hand; an estimated twenty perished while manning remote stations, which were tempting targets for Northern Paiutes unhappy with the increasing number of White settlers.

The riders' daring exploits immediately caught the attention of the American public. Newspapers and dime novels gushed with praise for the courage of the horsemen and for the efficiency of the mail delivery. However, its heyday would be short-lived. On October 24, 1861, the transcontinental telegraph was completed; a high-speed telegraph wire now linked the Atlantic and Pacific coasts. Nineteen months after its promising inaugural ride, the Pony Express was obsolete, done not only by technology's westward crawl but by the ambitious undertaking's staggering cost. The initial investments to establish stations were over $100,000, and expenses ran more than $30,000 per month. When operations ceased, the final tally registered a staggering loss of $200,000, the equivalent of over $6 million today. The Pony Express was history.

Despite the financial flop, and the service's short life span, the Pony Express nonetheless came to symbolize the can-do attitude of the American frontiersmen, and its riders are counted among the heroes of the mythical Wild West.

The Assassination of Jesse James

The most infamous and feared outlaw gang of the Old West was the James-Younger, whose most prominent members were the James brothers, Jesse and Frank, and the Younger brothers, Jim, John, Bob, and Cole. Led by the charismatic and self-promoting Jesse, the posse evolved out of the Civil War's bloody guerrilla warfare in Kansas and Missouri; most of the band's members had fought the Union under William Quantrill and William T. 'Bloody Bill' Anderson. Following the war, the former Confederates found a comfortable base of operations in Kentucky and Missouri, where locals perceived the gang's outlaw activities as a blow against Northern Reconstruction.

It has been estimated that in the decade following the end of the war, the outlaws had robbed a dozen banks, five trains, five stagecoaches, and the cash box of the ticket booth at the Kansas City Exposition. A sympathetic pro-Southern press hailed the outlaws as gallant soldiers of the Lost Cause of the Confederacy. Dime novels proclaimed Jesse James and his band as 'Robin Hoods of the West'. It was pure nonsense, the rebel bushwhackers no more than common thieves and cold-blooded killers, but the romanticized fiction sold papers and helped spread a truly American myth.

After nearly a decade of successful raids, the infamous gang's fortunes took a turn for the worse on September 7, 1876, when, straying from familiar and sympathetic Southern territory, it rode into Northfield, Minnesota to rob yet another bank. Things went awry from the start. The outlaws rode into town dressed in matching linen dusters, mounted on fine horseflesh, their prominence immediately drawing the attention of the wary Minnesotans. The outlaw lingered around town for a while, sizing things up, before springing into action in the mid-afternoon.

Jesse James (Library of Congress, LC-USZ262-38541)

The James brothers and another member of the crew went into the bank, while the others rode through town firing their guns, whooping it up in an effort to clear the streets and create a diversion. Rather than scatter, however, the already suspicious townsfolk, many of them Civil War veterans, went for their guns and commenced firing. They were not about to let their bank get robbed without a fight. The outlaws were soon under a hail of bullets.

Inside the bank, things didn't go much better. A stubborn, and undoubtedly brave, cashier refused to open the safe and was shot dead for his devotion. Just then, Cole Younger dashed into the bank and shouted to his partners they had to get going. The robbers fled into the chaos, only $26.75 richer for their trouble.

When the dust settled, two robbers, a bank employee, and a Northfield citizen were dead, and all of the surviving gang members had been wounded, except for Jesse, who had escaped unscathed.

The Minnesotans pursued the outlaws with a vengeance, organizing what is thought to be, to that time, the largest manhunt in US history. Two weeks after its formation, the posse caught up with the Youngers and Charlie Pitts, and a gunfight ensued. Pitts was killed, and the three Youngers, themselves severely wounded, surrendered and were sent to prison.

The James boys, who had split from the Youngers sometime during the retreat, somehow eluded capture, living to rob another day, a fact which only enhanced their already iconic image as the most charmed outlaws of the Old West. By escaping what newspapers had hailed as the most daring raid on record, Jesse and his legend, already part of Wild West folklore even before the botched robbery, grew even greater.

But the failure in Northfield, for all intents and purposes, ended the James-Younger Gang's reign of terror. Frank tried to settle into a normal, non-train-robbing life, but Jesse was not one for settling. He wanted back in business and accumulated new, but less reliable, associates in an attempt to resuscitate the good old days, a period of time that proved gone forever. On September 7, 1881, five years to the day after the Northfield debacle, Jesse and his new gang robbed their last train in Glendale, Missouri, the take a humiliating sum of just over $1,000.

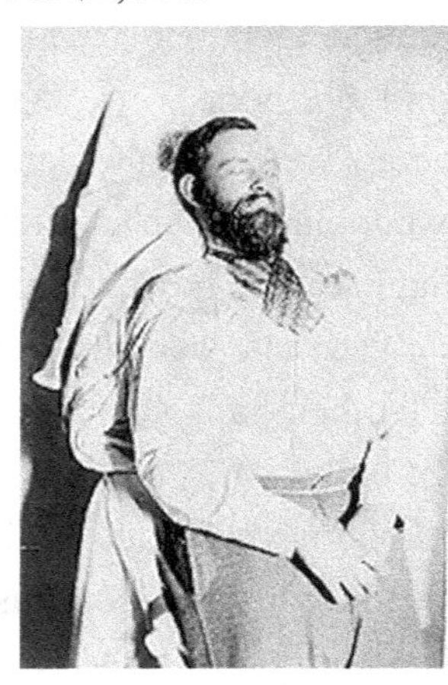

Jesse James Death Photo (Library of Congress, LC-USZ262-4255)

Shortly after, in the fall of 1881, Jesse, under the alias of Thomas Howard, moved with his wife and two young children from Kansas City to St. Joseph, Missouri, where he lived quietly until fate crossed the threshold of his small rented home on Lafayette Street. On April 3, 1882, the Howards hosted a pair of house guests: the newly minted partners in crime, the Ford brothers, Bob and Charlie. Over breakfast that morning, Jesse read the newspaper and noted the surrender to Missouri authorities of a former gang member, the disconcertingly named Dick Liddil, who was expected to implicate others in exchange for leniency. Jesse's harsh assessment that the traitor should be hung no doubt sent a chill down the spines of the Ford brothers, who had struck their own deal with the governor to bring in Jesse, dead or alive.

What happened next has puzzled many an Old West enthusiast. Jesse, complaining about the stifling heat, removed his jacket and gun belt, turned his back on the astonished Ford brothers, and mounted a chair to dust a framed needlepoint hanging on the wall. Bob Ford took quick advantage of his position. He pulled his.45-caliber revolver and emptied a single shot into the skull of the thirty-four-year-old desperado. Just like that, Jesse James, the most feared outlaw in the history of the Wild West, fell dead.

Bob Ford (National Archives)

WHAT HAPPENED NEXT?
St. Joseph

St. Joseph continued to grow and prosper into the twentieth century as a wholesale distribution center to the West. Its population peaked in 1900 at 100,000 residents. Today, St. Joseph is a small city of about 75,000.

Pony Express

Although its run was short-lived and its business model an untenable failure, the Pony Express is nevertheless firmly engrained in Old West culture as a symbol of frontier courage and tenacity. The lone rider facing off against harsh elements to bring civilization to the far West has been the subject of countless illustrations, books, and movies. The Pony Express even became a popular staple of Buffalo Bill Cody's Wild West show for thirty years, the reenactments touting the heroics of the riders well into the next century.

Jesse James

Jesse's widow, Zee, in order to support her two small children, resorted to selling off personal effects at a public auction. None of the family's possessions were safe; Jesse's dog even fetched $15. Zee also gave tours of the family home for ten cents, until she was evicted. The landlord then ran his own tours, upping the price to twenty-five cents and earning a hefty $1500 profit in a single year. Curious tourists chipped away pieces of furniture, walls, the floor, and even the picket fence.

The Ford brothers were arrested, indicted, and pled guilty to first-degree murder. They were immediately pardoned by Missouri Governor Thomas T. Crittenden, although the good governor balked at shelling out the $10,000 reward he'd placed on Jesse's head. The Fords fancied themselves heroes for slaying the most wanted man in the West and took their show on the road, hoping to cash in on their notoriety. Bob would perform on stage a reenactment of the murder, but nobody appreciated a man shooting another man, especially a man like the chivalrous Jesse James, in the back, and audiences proved unsympathetic. The Ford brothers were booed off the stage. When they received word that Frank James was stalking them, Charlie and Bob Ford's show-business careers officially ended.

Charlie committed suicide in 1884. Bob, always searching for his elusive fame, drifted throughout the West. In 1892, he landed in Creede, Colorado, where he was shot and killed in a saloon. But, while gone, he would not be forgotten. He is forever immortalized in the popular folk song *The Ballad of Jesse James*, as 'that dirty little coward that shot Mr. Howard, that laid poor Jesse James in his grave'. That these words cemented his legacy, when recognition and adoration were what he so desperately sought, maybe the harshest punishment Ford could have received for his crime.

Although the infamous outlaw was dead, the legend of Jesse James continued to grow. Indeed, for the next hundred years, countless books, movies, and television shows would portray Jesse as an almost mythical, gallant outlaw whose murders and robberies were somehow avenging a downtrodden South.

WHAT DO I DO WHEN I GET THERE?

St. Joseph has several museums that preserve its layered ties to the Old West.

Pony Express Museum

Pony Express National Museum, 914 Penn Street, St. Joseph, Missouri (ponyexpress.org)

Housed in what was originally the wooden St. Joseph Pikes Peak Stables, the museum features photographs, scale models, documents, and artifacts, all of which illustrate the brief but culturally significant history of the Pony Express.

A life-sized display recaptures the moment when young Johnny Fry left the very building you are standing in to begin the first leg of the perilous two-thousand-mile journey to deliver mail to Sacramento. There is a short film detailing the daunting logistics and physical hardships of the ambitious undertaking, as well as a detailed sixty-foot diorama of the route, along with exhibits of a relay station and a harness and tack shop. Although some modern historians are skeptical of Buffalo Bill Cody's experience as a Pony Express rider, there is no doubt in St. Joseph.

The museum's most compelling feature is that it is situated in the original stables. Through the decades, obvious improvements have been made, like encasing the structure in brick, but you can view preserved excavations, which include the original well for the stables and other artifacts from the nineteenth century.

Patee House Museum, 202 Penn Street, St. Joseph, Missouri, (ponyexpressjessejames.com)

The impressive four-story hotel built in 1858 is now a world-class museum holding a diverse array of nineteenth and early twentieth-century artifacts. The building itself owns an interesting history. It not only served as headquarters for the Pony Express but also as the US provost marshal's office and as the Federal recruiting office during the Civil War. Zee James, Jesse's widow, even stayed in the hotel the night of her husband's slaying.

Patee House Museum

Nineteenth-century replica stores, with original artifacts, are spread throughout the museum's two floors. One such exhibit is of a dentist's office,

complete with dental instruments, belonging to St. Joseph's own Dr. Walter L. Cronkite Sr., father of the famed newscaster Walter Cronkite (there is a Walter Cronkite Memorial exhibit located at nearby Missouri Western State University).

Another interesting replica is that of a nineteenth-century mortician's

Patee Museum Exhibit

workspace, complete with period caskets and a horse-drawn hearse.

Among the old cars, trucks, fire engines, stagecoaches, and trains sit some unique items tied to the James boys, such as Jesse's shaving mug and Frank's shoes. There is also a Buffalo Soldier exhibit, which includes the West Point Cadet uniform of Lt. Flipper, the first African American to graduate from the USMA. A great museum.

James House Museum

Jesse James Home Museum-1202, Penn Street, St. Joseph, Missouri

This is it. The very place where Jesse James's life ended at the hands of Robert Ford. Kind of. The house has been moved from its original location, a short walk from the museum and marked with a memorial stone, at 1318 Lafayette Street a couple times and, since 1977, has been on the grounds of the Patee House Museum. The small, one-story James House Museum house is now a museum, too, and the parlor, where the killing took place, is set up to look as it did when Jesse met his maker on April 3, 1882.

Prominently displayed below the replica 'God Bless This House' needlepoint is a large hole in the wall, presumably from the bullet that passed through Jesse's skull. The size of the hole, however, looks today like Jesse was shot by a cannon, since souvenir hunters have for years pecked away and enlarged the cavity.

God Bless This House

The small room next to the parlor is dedicated to displaying items associated with the exhuming of Jesse's corpse in 1995. Periodically, in the decades following Jesse's demise, impostors would come forward and declare themselves the real Jesse James, casting doubt on the story of Jesse's death at Ford's hand. To put an end to the historical debate once and for all, it was decided to dig Jesse up for testing. DNA was extracted from his corpse's tooth and compared with samples from living known relatives. The good news is the testing confirmed, to within a 99.7% certainty, that it was indeed Jesse's remains in the grave.

The bad news is his skull had a bullet entrance but not an exit wound. You don't have to be a coroner to conclude the fatal bullet never left Jesse's skull. But what about the ever-expanding crater in the wall of the old Howard house? Regardless of reality's intrusion on their legend, the museum's staff remain quite proud of the hole; a prominent sign in front of the house lures visitors to 'see the bullet hole'.

The exhumation room also features remnants of what was left of Jesse's coffin—fragments of wood, shattered glass from the lid, and wooden handles. The showpiece of the display, however, is a replica of Jesse's skull, complete with a lone bullet hole. Also displayed are items recovered from the coffin, including a tie stick pin, a bullet believed to have been in Jesse's lung since the Civil War, and a scattering of stubby, heavily stained teeth, for which the museum offers the following explanation: Jesse James, the outlaw who robbed many a train and killed many a man, may have also ground his teeth at night. It is a pretty cool museum, all in all.

WHERE CAN I WET MY WHISTLE?

First Ward House, 2101 Saint Joseph Ave., St. Joseph, Missouri

Built in 1878 to accommodate train crews, it soon became a popular stopping-off point for weary settlers heading West. It was located in the city's first voting ward, thus the name. It proudly proclaims itself the oldest bar west of the Mississippi, and it is rumored that the infamous Bonnie and Clyde were among its patrons. In the 1950s, the original four-story structure was shortened to two stories, and the bricks removed were utilized in the expanding Pony Express Museum. Regrettably, in 2015, a devastating fire ravished the building, destroying a lot of the original furnishings, but the sturdy long bar was preserved.

First Ward House

Today, it is a happening nightspot in the evening hours, with live music and a spacious outdoor patio covered by a large awning that, unfortunately, makes it look like an airplane hangar. The Old West ambiance is gone, but the food is decent—natives rave about the wings—and it is, after all, the oldest bar west of Old Man River. Just go with it.

WHAT ABOUT GRUB?

J.C. Wyatt House, 1309 Hall Street, St. Joseph, Missouri (jcwyatt.net)
The hours are quirky, reservations are required, and you have to order your food forty-eight hours in advance. But a meal includes a tour of the 1891 Victorian mansion. Not for everybody, but it's probably one of the best restaurants in the city.

Cabbage Roll, 2641 Lafayette Street, St. Joseph, Missouri

Nothing fancy, but quaint and homey. Specializing in German and Ukrainian fare, it is known among the locals for its signature dish—what else? The German-style cabbage roll.

WHERE CAN I HANG MY HAT AND PUT MY BOOTS UNDER A BED?

St. Joseph is a college town, so there are plenty of run-of-the-mill chain motels downtown (Ramada Inn, Days Inn, Holiday Inn Express, etc.). If you're looking for a little atmosphere, however, there are a couple of B&Bs to consider.

Whiskey Mansion B&B, 1723 Francis Street, St. Joseph, Missouri (whiskeymansion1885.com)

Conveniently located near the museums, the updated Victorian was originally built in 1885 for a whiskey baron. It is beautifully decorated with nineteenth-century furnishings.

Shakespeare Chateau, 809 Hall Street, St. Joseph, Missouri (shakespearechateau.com)

Another Victorian was first built in 1885. This, too, is complete with nineteenth-century décor.

IS THERE ANYTHING ELSE?

When the alias Mr. Howard attempted a new life in St. Joseph, he did not wander too far from the family farm in Kearney, Missouri. About an hour away from St. Joseph, on I-29, on the way back to Kansas City, lies the James family farm.

Jesse James Farm & Museum, 2126 Jesse James Farm Road, Kearney, Missouri

The museum plays visitors a short film and displays an impressive collection of James family artifacts, including Jesse's boots and spurs. Especially compelling is the wicker chair that Jesse stood on and the feather duster he held when he was gunned down.

A short walk down the hill from the

Jesse James Farm and Museum

museum leads to the James family home, where Frank and Jesse were raised, and where Frank lived the last years of his life. The home remained in the James family until the 1950s when it was turned over to Clay County. At one point, the house fell into such disrepair that it was taken apart and painstakingly reconstructed, preserving as many of the original pieces as possible. A guide walks you through the house, pointing out the original furnishings and recounting interesting tidbits from the history of the James family. For example, Jesse married a girl with the same name as his mother: Zerelda. One might find this a little peculiar, given the name's uniqueness, but it's not really the odd part: his wife was named specifically after Jesse's mother, who happened to be her aunt. Think about that.

On a more somber note, the family homestead was the site of a disaster in the early morning hours of January 26, 1875. Pinkerton detectives, believing Jesse and Frank were inside, threw some type of incendiary device into the home in a misguided attempt to smoke out the outlaws. The firebomb ended up in a fireplace, causing an explosion that killed Jesse's half-brother Archie and maimed his strong-willed mother. The botched Pinkerton raid increased sympathy for the James boys, not only in the South but throughout the country as well.

After Jesse's death, he was buried in the front yard, and his mother, exhibiting the family's entrepreneurial spirit, gave tours of the home and sold stones from her son's grave, which she constantly replaced, for twenty-five cents. Today, the museum gift shop still sells the stones for the same price. I bought one but made the tour guide take it directly from the creek, behind the homestead, and place it on the grave—I'm no sucker.

James Grave

Jesse James gravesite, Mt. Olivet Cemetery, 101 Missouri 92, Kearney, Missouri

In 1902, Jesse's remains were reinterred at the family plot in the local cemetery, right in town, at the Mt. Olivet Cemetery. A map at the cemetery notes the grave's easy-to-find location.

The Jesse James Bank Museum, 103 N. Water Street, Liberty, Missouri

Ten miles outside of Kearney, in Liberty, stands the formerly named Clay County Savings Association. On February 18, 1866, approximately twelve desperadoes, a group that would ultimately evolve into the notorious James-Younger Gang, pulled off the nation's first daytime bank robbery, leaving one innocent bystander dead and the outlaws $60,000 richer. Visitors can look into the original vault into which the robbers herded the startled tellers and peruse artifacts, pictures, and documents associated with the daring robbery.

If your curiosity about the Pony Express was piqued by your visit to St. Joseph, you can drive modern highways that approximate or closely parallel the historic route taken by those adventurous riders a century and a half ago. The National Park Service has marked the highways and offers downloadable maps outlining the route through eight states: www.nps.gov/poes/planyourvisit/directions.htm

WHAT SHOULD I READ AND WATCH BEFORE I HIT THE TRAIL?

BOOKS

- *The Saga of the Pony Express* (2002, by Joseph DiCerto)—a detailed and entertaining history, complete with maps and appendixes of riders' relay stations.
- *Orphans Preferred: The Twisted Truth and Lasting Legend of the Pony Express* (2003, by Christopher Corbett)—the author examines the various myths that have evolved from the nineteen-month Pony Express.
- *West Like Lightning: The Brief Legendary Ride of the Pony Express* (2018, by Jim DeFelice)—fast-paced, comprehensive history of the short-lived experiment.
- *Frank and Jesse James: The Story Behind the Legend* (2000, by Ted P. Yeatman)—extensively researched examination of the lives of the West's most famous brothers.
- *Jesse James Was His Name; Or, Fact, and Fiction Concerning the Careers of the Notorious James Brothers of Missouri* (1966, by William A. Settle Jr.)—the author separates fact from fiction in exploring the eventful life of Missouri's violent son.

VIDEOS

- *Pony Express* (1953, Paramount)—Charlton Heston as Buffalo Bill and Forrest Tucker as Wild Bill Hickok ride through bad weather and Indian attacks to deliver the mail to California.

- *The Assignation of Jesse James by the Coward Robert Ford* (2007, Warner Home Video)—Brad Pitt as Jesse (albeit with bright white smiling teeth), and Casey Affleck as Bob Ford are both outstanding in this dark, historically accurate portrayal of the infamous outlaw's last days. A bonus is Sam Shepard's underplayed performance as Frank.
- *The Last Days of Frank and Jesse James* (1986, Warner Home Video)—Country music stars dominate the screen, with Kris Kristofferson as Jesse, Johnny Cash as Frank and, in an odd bit of casting, June Carter Cash, Johnny's wife, as their feisty mother. Willie Nelson also makes an entertaining appearance as Confederate General Joseph Shelby.

TIPS FROM THE TRAIL

You can definitely spend a couple days hitting the museums in St. Joseph, Kearney, and Liberty. The James Farm and Museum is particularly compelling, partly because the surrounding countryside remains as it did when the James boys roamed its rolling hills over a century ago (and the twenty-five cents stones are a nice touch). A traveling option is to stay in nearby Kansas City, only about an hour and a half away, and make a couple day trips to the museums. You can't beat the K.C. barbeque.

Frank—The Law-Abiding James Boy

In 1882, Frank James, desiring a different fate than his younger brother's, decided to try his luck in court. The outlaw, still very much wanted for his crimes, surrendered his pistol to Missouri's Governor Crittenden, ceremoniously noting that 'no living man, except myself, has been permitted to touch [the gun] since 1861'... He was tried for armed robbery, twice in Missouri and once in Alabama, but his peers found him not guilty each time. The State of Missouri refused to extradite Frank to Minnesota, where a Northern jury would have, no doubt, rendered a much different verdict.

Four years after he surrendered, Frank walked out of jail a free man. Frank considered himself a family man—he had a wife and young son—and he was determined not to end up behind bars. He roamed Missouri, Tennessee, and Oklahoma, taking on various jobs, including shoe salesman, berry picker, and Burlesque-show ticket taker. He even joined up with his former partner in crime, Cole Younger, and toured the South as part of a Wild West show. He ultimately retired to the family farm in Kearney, giving tours and posing for pictures with curious tourists (for a fee of course). The

Frank James (National Archives)

former outlaw passed away quietly of a stroke on February 15, 1915, at the age of seventy-two.

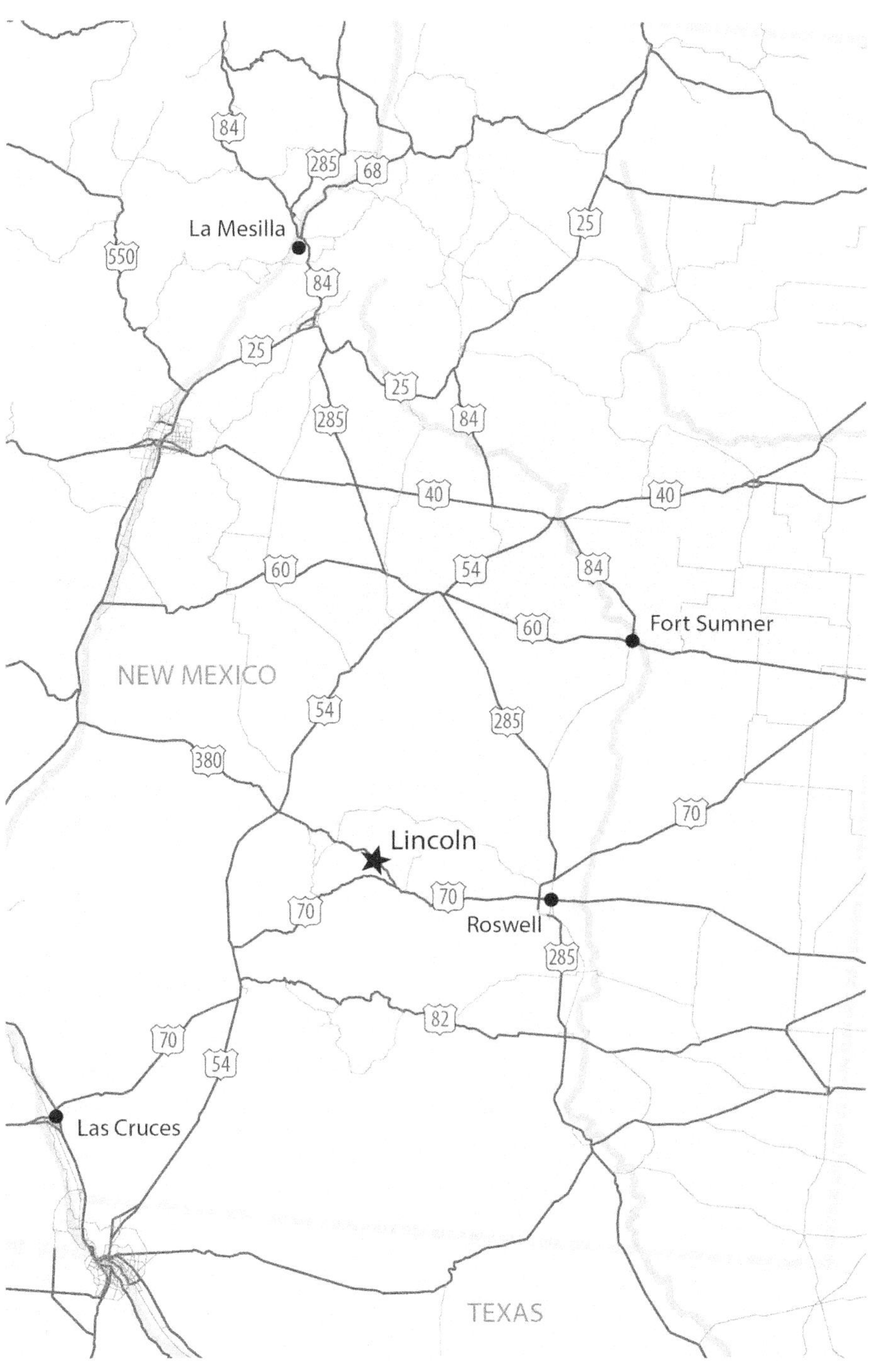
84
285
68
25
La Mesilla
550
84
25
25
285
84
40
40
60
54
84
60
Fort Sumner
NEW MEXICO
54
285
70
380
70
Lincoln
70
70
Roswell
70
285
82
70
54
Las Cruces
TEXAS

Lincoln

New Mexico

Chuck Knudsen/ Wikimedia Commons/ CC BY-SA 4.0 Deed | Attribution-ShareAlike 4.0 International | Creative Commons

WHAT HAPPENED HERE?

On April 28, 1881, twenty-one-year-old Billy the Kid was being held upstairs in the Lincoln County Courthouse for the murder of Sheriff William Brady when he managed to escape and elude the gallows. The Kid's bold jailbreak left behind two dead deputies but cemented his reputation and enduring legacy as the most engaging outlaw of the Old West.

Located in the desolate southeastern corner of New Mexico, the small village of La Placita was renamed Lincoln when it became the capital of the newly formed Lincoln County in 1869. At the time, Lincoln County was the largest county in the United States, measuring a hundred seventy miles north to south and a hundred fifty from east to west.

In the fall of 1877, trouble was brewing in the arid ranges of the Pecos Valley of southeast New Mexico between two factions vying for political and economic control of Lincoln County. One faction was headed by the 'King of the Pecos', John H. Chisum, who controlled over a hundred thousand head of cattle on a range a hundred fifty miles long.

John Chisum

Chisum's ever-increasing herds became targets for rustlers, and the self-made cattle baron was not about to put up with cattle thieves. In 1875, an ambitious rival to Chisum's empire emerged in Lincoln: former army Major Lawrence G. Murphy. Although the Irish immigrant could not compete with Chisum's cattle enterprise, he made his money as a middleman, supplying beef to the army through lucrative government contracts. Murphy was also putting an economic squeeze on Chisum, and other ranchers, by establishing a general store, a flour mill, and a hotel in Lincoln.

Aligned with Chisum were Murphy's former attorney, Alexander McSween, and British rancher John H. Tunstall. Siding with Murphy was fellow Irishman James J. Dolan, who ran the Murphy store, an impressive two-story structure, dubbed *The House*. For muscle, The House employed the deadly Jesse Evans and his gang.

Chisum suspected The House was fulfilling its government contracts with his beef, but he was frustrated in his attempts to seek legal remedies since Murphy owned the law in Lincoln, including Sheriff William Brady, and had powerful allies in the territorial capital of Santa Fe.

As if on cue, into this fire rode an eighteen-year-old calling himself William H. Bonney.

Starting life as Henry McCarty in the Irish slums on New York City's Lower East Side, by the time he arrived in New Mexico he had taken the name Bonney but was known throughout the southwest as 'the Kid', a good-natured, charismatic horse thief and gambler. And despite his tender age and crooked, buck-toothed smile, he was also known as a man to be reckoned with. The Kid aligned himself with Chisum and was hired by John Henry Tunstall.

Billy was no cow puncher; he was there to prevent cattle rustling. He developed a surprisingly close relationship with the natty Brit, who took a liking to the engaging youngster. Billy came to look upon Tunstall as a mentor, although the transplanted rancher was only twenty-four years old.

Murphy (seated) and Dolan

The only authenticated photograph of Billy the kid.

In a mind-numbingly convoluted set of facts, proceeds from a life insurance policy intertwined with an estate being handled by McSween, Murphy had obtained an attachment on McSween's aasets. Somewhat inexplicitly the House-controlled Sheriff William Brady determined that the attachment included Tunstall's stock and horses. On February 18, 1878, Brady dispatched deputies to the Tunstall ranch located on the Rio Feliz to levy the attachment. Along the way, they ran into Tunstall, who was traveling alone on his way into Lincoln.

Not one for conciliatory dialogue, the band simply shot him down. The cold-blooded murder of the Englishman sparked what would be known as the Lincoln County War. Although prior to coming to Lincoln, while Billy had killed men here and there, the slaying of the inoffensive and highly respected Tunstall propelled Billy into a killing spree from which there would be no return. The Kid's fate as an outlaw destined to meet a violent end was sealed.

The Kid joined a posse calling itself the Regulators. The group vowed to hunt down Tunstall's killers, and Billy soon unleashed his vengeance. After a three-day ride, the Regulators captured two Murphy men, but Billy had no interest in taking prisoners. The Kid and another Regulator shot and killed the hapless prisoners before they reached Lincoln. They also killed one of their own men when he unwisely attempted to stop Billy, who was just getting started.

Henry Tunstall

Sheriff William Brady sought to arrest Billy but had trouble locating him, although the elusive Kid was seeking refuge in the Tunstall store, right on Lincoln's Main Street. Billy wasn't big on hiding. On April 1, 1878, Billy and some of the Regulators stood behind an adobe wall next to the Tunstall store and opened fire on Brady and two of his deputies as they were walking across the street from the courthouse.

The men exchanged gunfire, and the sheriff fell dead. With guns still blazing, Billy walked into the street and retrieved a rifle, which Brady had confiscated from Billy two weeks before, from the sheriff's death grip. Billy obtained a slight wound for his trouble, but he got his rifle back. His boldness under fire only added to his reputation as a brash but charmed gunfighter.

The Lincoln County War reached a violent climax a few months later on July 15, 1878, when Billy and fellow Regulators barricaded themselves in McSween's adobe home in the center of Lincoln.

The House faction positioned themselves in nearby buildings, and the factions exchanged gunfire for the next five days before the Regulators were burned out of the McSween home. Billy and the others, facing heavy gunfire, attempted to escape through the back door of the burning house. Once again, Billy escaped, but McSween and four others were not so lucky; they were cut down coming out of the doorway. With both Tunstall and McSween dead, the Lincoln County War was over, and the Regulators, including Billy, dispersed into the countryside.

Gov. Lew Wallace

In the fall of 1878, a new territorial governor was appointed, former Union General, and future author of 'Ben Hur', Lew Wallace. Wallace was charged with the task of cleaning up the Lincoln County mess, and he immediately sought to prosecute those responsible for the killings. Word reached Wallace that the War's most infamous participant, Billy the Kid, wanted to meet; the outlaw was willing to give potentially incriminating testimony against The House in exchange for amnesty.

In March 1879, the Kid actually met with Wallace. The details of the meeting are lost to history, but Billy walked away from the parley believing he was to be given amnesty in exchange for his testimony implicating other participants in the Lincoln County War. The Kid was placed in custody, on a bogus charge, and did testify, but the ambitious new governor reneged on his promise. Predictably, Billy escaped custody and left Lincoln County for the friendlier environs of Ft. Sumner, New Mexico. The popular Kid was a wanted man, but, at least initially, nobody in New Mexico seemed anxious to catch him. Billy spent the summer and autumn of 1879 making a nuisance of himself by rustling cattle and, never one to shy from a fight, killing a man in a saloon altercation in January 1880.

Alexander McSween

Billy's outlaw exploits were beginning to be followed in the Eastern press, whose readership became enthralled with the young, brazen 'Billy the Kid'. Santa Fe politicos were not as smitten with Billy's open flaunting of authority, which painted the territory as a lawless frontier, which was neither good for business nor the Territory's bid for statehood.

By the fall of 1880, there was a new sheriff in town. Pat Garrett, a tall, lanky ex-buffalo hunter, with Chisum's enthusiastic backing, was elected Sheriff of Lincoln County and immediately set his sights on the pesky but deadly Kid.

It didn't take the new sheriff very long. On the night of December 22, Garrett and his posse tracked the Kid and some of his gang to an abandoned rock house at a wisp of a town named Stinking Springs, east of Fort Sumner. The Kid did not give up without a fight, but when one of his closest friends was shot and killed, he relented and was taken alive.

Garrett took his prize prisoner to Santa Fe, where Billy cooled his heels in jail for three months awaiting trial for the murder of Sheriff Brady. The Kid spent his time firing off a series of letters to Governor Wallace desperately pleading for the amnesty he was promised and giving newspaper interviews.

In April 1881, Billy was taken to Mesilla, a small town south of Santa Fe, where he was tried and promptly convicted of the killing of Sheriff Brady. The only man convicted of any crime in the bloody Lincoln War, he was then sentenced to hang. It was determined that Billy would meet his maker at the scene of his deadly crime: Lincoln.

Billy was transported back to Lincoln, where he was held upstairs in the courthouse building, which had once been Murphy and Dolan's mercantile store. Billy was confined in a large room that had once been Murphy's bedroom, situated next to Garrett's office. The newly minted Sheriff genuinely liked Billy, which contributed to a series of missteps that would have deadly consequences. The sympathetic Garrett, overly concerned with the Kid's comfort, determined the Kid need not be constrained with short-chained shackles, opting for a less-restraining long-chained version. Then on April 27, Garrett left town on other business.

That Garrett could possibly have had more pressing law enforcement obligations over ensuring Billy the Kid kept his appointment with the hangman is a head-scratcher. Nonetheless, depart Lincoln he did, leaving two deputies, Bob Olinger, and J.W. Bell, in charge of one of the deadliest outlaws of the

Old West. Although Deputies Olinger and Bell seemed blissfully unaware they were dangerously overmatched, the Kid certainly was not.

Adding to the deputies' impending peril was Olinger's habit of poking Billy in the chest with a loaded ten-gauge shotgun and verbally taunting him, something he'd done since Mesilla. In historical retrospect, it is difficult to conjure up a worse person to bully than Billy the Kid, who would soon have his revenge.

On the evening of April 28, Olinger escorted five other prisoners across the street for dinner at the Wortley Hotel. The Kid, left alone with Bell, saw his opportunity and asked the deputy to take him outside to use the privy. Coming back from the outhouse, they both started to climb the narrow stairs when the Kid overpowered the hapless Bell. The Kid managed to get Bell's pistol and shot him in the back as he ran down the stairs. Bell crashed through the back door and fell dead in the dusty courthouse yard.

Billy wriggled out of his handcuffs, grabbed Olinger's shotgun from Garett's office, and took a position at the small upstairs window on the eastern side of the building overlooking the sideyard. Olinger, upon hearing the gunshot that slayed Bell, hurried from the Wortley toward the courthouse. He got to the side yard, looked up to the small window, and gazed upon his final scene: a smiling Billy holding a shotgun. "Hello, Bob," he heard before he felt the devastating blast from both barrels of his own shotgun. The Kid smashed the shotgun against the windowsill and threw it beside his dying tormentor. Billy danced a little jig, much to the bemusement of the astonished onlookers, 'borrowed' a horse (which was returned a couple days later), rode out of Lincoln, and, as eloquently phrased by noted historian Dr. Paul H. Hutton, 'he rode not to freedom but into immortality'.

Garrett pursued Billy, who wasn't that difficult to find; the Kid didn't like to stray from familiar surroundings. Billy was fluent in Spanish, and his outgoing and friendly personality made him a favorite among the locals, especially the señoritas. On July 13, 1881, Garrett and two deputies rode into Fort Sumner to investigate rumblings that the Kid was in the vicinity. Around midnight on July 14, Garrett entered the home of rancher Pete Maxwell to inquire about the Kid. It was suspected that Billy had a romantic relationship with Maxwell's younger sister, Paulita.

In fact, it was rumored at the time that Paulita was pregnant with Billy's child. In any event, Garrett, leaving his two deputies on the porch, was talking with Maxwell in his bedroom when in walked Billy the Kid. Billy asked why there were men outside, and Garrett opened fire in the darkened bedroom, striking the Kid in the chest. Within minutes, the most engaging outlaw of the Old West was dead.

WHAT HAPPENED NEXT?

Although the names John Chisum and Lawrence Murphy are closely associated with the Lincoln County War, neither of them took an active role in any of the gunplay. Murphy was mortally ill at the time and finally succumbed to cancer and alcoholism, at the age of forty-seven, on October 20, 1878.

During the War, Chisum had supported McSween but shrewdly kept himself, and his men, out of the dirty work. After the War, Chisum continued to prosper, and in 1881, built a hundred-fifty-foot-long adobe 'Long House' at his South Spring Ranch, 'Jinglebob'. The 'King of the Pecos' didn't enjoy it very long, however. He developed tumors on his neck and would travel to Eureka Springs, Arkansas, for treatments, where he died on December 22, 1884, at the age of sixty. His business interests were turned over to his brothers, but they were not John Chisum, and by 1891 the Jinglebob Ranch was no more.

In 1879, James Dolan was tried for killing two participants in the War but was acquitted, having raised the successful defense of being drunk at the time. He acquired Tunstall's ranch, stayed involved in politics, and was elected to the Territorial Senate in 1888. He died on February 26, 1898, at the age of forty-nine, of—what else?—alcoholism.

Alexander McSween's widow, Susan, seems to have fared the best out of the Lincoln County War fraternity. With assets accumulated from her late husband's estate and cattle given to her by John Chisum, she started a ranch in the Three Rivers area, well away from Lincoln. She prospered as a rancher, got married and divorced, and became known as the 'Cattle Queen of New Mexico'. She died in White Oaks, New Mexico, in 1931, at the age of eighty-six.

Almost before William Bonney's body was cold, widely popular dime novels began to describe Billy the Kid's exaggerated outlaw exploits in a sympathetic light, painting Billy as a quick-shooting outlaw with boyish charisma. Pat Garrett wanted to set the record straight, however, and teamed up with journalist Ash Upton to publish An Authentic Life of Billy the Kid.

The product was anything but an authentic biography of the Kid, but it did portray him in a romanticized light, a depiction that propelled Billy's already well-known outlaw reputation to a new level.

Garrett's fanciful biography of the Kid.

Pat Garrett was hailed as a hero for having slain the notorious Kid. Billy still had his sympathizers, however, and Garrett couldn't get reelected in New Mexico until 1899. Garrett served a stint as a Texas Ranger, and in 1901, President Teddy Roosevelt appointed him to the lucrative position of United States Customs Collector at El Paso, Texas. President Roosevelt did not reappoint Garrett during his second term, though, and in 1905 he returned to New Mexico, where he tried his hand at ranching but spent a considerable amount of his time drinking and gambling. On February 29, 1905, on a desolate stretch of road, a few miles east of Las Cruces, New Mexico, the great lawman was shot in the back of the head while relieving himself on the side of the road (see p. 169). The circumstances surrounding the killing are still shrouded in mystery but thus ended the life of the killer of Billy the Kid.

In the mid-twentieth century, the Western was the most popular genre of film and television, and Billy the Kid characters were frequently and prominently featured. It has been estimated that Billy the Kid has had an eminent role in over seventy-five films, where he is often portrayed as a charming, misunderstood, but deadly youth fighting a corrupt system.

Into the twenty-first century, Billy the Kid continues to be a popular subject for magazines and novels, and the Kid is still deeply ingrained in the American psyche as an embodiment of the daring and courage required to tame the Wild West; although, ironically, he was one of the reasons the West was Wild. In 2010, outgoing New Mexico Governor Bill Richardson, admittedly allured by the romanticism of the enduring legend of Billy the Kid, seriously considered granting a posthumous pardon to the slayer of Sheriff Brady. The descendants of Pat Garrett, concerned that a pardon would taint the reputation of their lawman relative, lobbied hard against the pardon, arguing the Kid was an 'incorrigible killer'. The descendants of Governor Wallace also chimed in, calling the consideration of such a pardon 'nonsense'. The governor, announcing his decision on ABC's Good Morning America, acknowledged the Kid was 'good for tourism' but, nonetheless, denied the pardon, reasoning there was "historical ambiguity as to why Governor Wallace reneged on his pardon."

The allure and popularity of the Old West's most charismatic outlaw show no signs of waning. In 2011, the only authenticated photograph of Billy the Kid sold at auction for a whopping $2.3 million. Not surprisingly, the astonishing sales price sparked a sudden appearance of photos ostensibly featuring the Kid, including one in which the most feared badman in the West is playing a genteel game of croquet. None of the recently discovered images, however, have been authenticated by historians and facial recognition 'experts'. But that doesn't mean there isn't one out there somewhere in somebody's attic. Happy hunting!

WHAT DO I DO WHEN I GET THERE?

Lincoln, New Mexico is an Old West enthusiast's treasure trove, seemingly frozen in the 1870s.

Unlike other authentic Old West towns, the original adobe structures have managed to avoid fire and subsequent touristy reconstruction. Seventeen structures and other outbuildings have survived the 1878 Lincoln County War. Although it is not a ghost town, it's close. It's about a three-hour drive from Las Cruces and has one street (Route 380), which President Rutherford B. Hayes once called 'the most dangerous street in America'.

The infamous narrow stairway.

Possibly the most famous bullet hole in the history of the West.

Tunstall Store

On that now-quiet half-mile street, running through the middle of town, it has been estimated that over fifty people were killed between 1868 and 1882.

At the north end of town stands The House, the Murphy-Dolan store, which was converted to the courthouse from where Billy the Kid made his deadly escape.

The impressive two-story structure looks as it did in 1878 and houses a museum. The historical displays include a letter written by the Kid to Governor Wallace pleading for amnesty. You can walk up the narrow stairway where Billy overpowered Deputy Bell, gaze upon a hole in the wall reportedly made by Billy's bullet, and look out the small upstairs window where Billy set his deadly sights on Olinger.

On the east side of the street, directly across from The House, stands the Wortley Hotel, where Deputy Olinger partook of his last earthly meal.

The Tunstall Store, further down the street, also appears as it did in the late nineteenth century, and includes 1880s merchandise in the original shelving and cases.

A small room in the back of the store is where Billy hid after killing Sheriff Brady. An empty lot beside the store is where the McSween home once stood, before being burned to the ground by the Murphy-Dolan faction.

Down the street from the Tunstall Store is the Torreon, a thirty-foot stone defensive tower built by Hispanic settlers in the 1860s for protection from the Apache.

Tunstall Death Site

Farther south is the more modern Lincoln County Historical Center, which displays artifacts and pictures related to the Lincoln county war and Apache history,

Outside of town, in the Lincoln National Forest, about four miles off Route 70, Forrest Road 443 then Forest Trail 9019D will lead you to the death site of Henry Tunstall.

Unfortunately, nothing remains of Chisum's Jinglebob Ranch. The area that was once the site of the great cattle ranch replaced by industrial agriculture. In Roswell sits the Chisum's South Springs Historical Marker on Route 380 and South Main. If you drive about four miles southeast of Roswell, just below the South Springs River, you can gaze upon the actual site of the forgotten ranch.

Lincoln Courthouse

IS THERE ANYTHING ELSE?

Smokey Bear Museum and Grave, 118 W. Smokey Bear Blvd., Capitan, New Mexico

In 1950, a bear cub was rescued from a forest fire in the New Mexico Lincoln National Forest, and the rest is history. When the icon of the National Park Service passed away in 1976, he was returned home for burial.

If you somehow find yourself in Lincoln, New Mexico, you should venture out and see the other sites linked to the Old West's most famous outlaw. You're in the midst of Billy the Kid country, after all.

LA MESILLA, NEW MEXICO:

Located about two hundred miles southwest of Lincoln lies the site of Billy's trial for the murder of Sheriff Brady. Founded in 1848, La Mesilla was the social and transportation center of southern New Mexico in the Kid's Day and, during the Civil War, was the capital of the short-lived Confederate Territory of Arizona.

Where Billy the Kid was tried

The old courthouse building still stands, but, unfortunately, it is now a souvenir shop, where there is seemingly no limit to the variety of Billy the Kid items one can purchase.

Looking past the cheesy t-shirt shops, La Mesilla is a quaint old Mexican Village with some upscale artsy shops and a Village Plaza that frequently hosts outdoor markets.

LAS CRUCES, NEW MEXICO:

Lying five miles to the south of La Mesilla, Las Cruces ultimately replaced the old village as the cultural hub of southern New Mexico when it became a stop on the Santa Fe Railway in 1881.

Death site of Pat Garrett: There is a highway marker on Route 70, a few miles east of Las Cruces, at Jornada Rd., indicating the death site of Pat Garrett is near. The actual site however is located about a mile from the marker, in the desert, behind Organ Mountain High School.

To get there, continue east on Route 70, get off at the Mesa Grande exit, and make a right onto the first street. On your left, you will notice a dirt road before reaching the Mesa Grande housing subdivision. If you don't have a four-wheel drive, park your car dead site. here and walk south along the road.

As you walk south, you will see some large power lines on the left (to the east) and some smaller power lines to the right (west). Follow the smaller power lines south—a bumpy dirt road runs beneath them. You will walk into Alameda Arroyo and will soon approach a steep rise to the south. The death marker is located on this beaten dirt road just under one of the power line poles.

If you go in the summer, watch for rattlesnakes and bring sufficient water (or your beverage of choice). I estimate approximately a thirty-minute hike from the main road. GPS Coordinates are 32.366203 N, -106.717152 W.

FORT SUMNER, NEW MEXICO:

It's a bit of a hike from Lincoln, about two hours north but well worth the trip. Unfortunately, the actual town is long gone, but Billy the Kid is buried there, somewhere. I'll explain. On July 15, 1881, The Kid's body was placed in a wooden casket and interred at the Fort Sumner military cemetery, next to his former compadres, Tom O'Folliard and Charlie Bowdre. A simple wooden marker was placed at the head of the grave, but through the years the marker disappeared, partly because the locals used it for target practice.

Over the decades, the nearby Pecos River flooded, with floodwaters occasionally carrying away headstones and even caskets. By 1937, Billy the Kid was lying in an unmarked grave. Four surviving pallbearers were called upon to locate the gravesite. They couldn't agree among themselves, so they placed a cement marker approximately in the middle of the four different selections. That marker was swept away in 1945, along with some more graves, in yet another flood, in 1945.

Today, Billy's grave is behind the Old Fort Sumner Museum (3501 Billy the Kid Rd., Fort Sumner, NM), surrounded by a big iron cage to prevent the stealing of the headstone, a crime that has happened more than once over the decades. The museum, unfortunately, closed, and its artifacts were auctioned off in 2017. Down the road is a Billy the Kid Museum (1435 East Sumner Ave., Fort Sumner, NM 88119, (505)355-2942), which has some original artifacts associated with the Kid, such as his saddle.

WHERE CAN I WET MY WHISTLE?

You are out of luck in Lincoln. Unless you're staying at the hotel (see below), it's going to be a dry afternoon. If you're in **Mesilla**, you have a couple of good options.

Double Eagle, 2355 Calle De Guadalupe, Mesilla, NM 88046 (575)523-6700 (double-eagle-mesilla.com)

Located on the Plaza in historic Old Mesilla, the building dates back to 1849. The building went through several reincarnations but was turned into a bar/restaurant in 1970. It has a great thirty-foot hand-carved oak and walnut bar, complete with a brass rail, dating back to Billy the Kid. Pretty good steak, and, oh yeah, the place is haunted.

El Patio Cantina, 2171 Calle De Parian, Mesilla, NM 88046 (575)526-9943

The building has been in the same family (Fountain) for over hundred fifty years and has been a watering hole since 1933. In the late 1800s, it was a post office, so Billy may have walked through its doors to mail a letter. Clearly a dive bar, but there is nothing wrong with that.

WHAT ABOUT GRUB?

CAPITAN

Food is really limited to the Dolan House and the Wortley Hotel, both of which are quite good. If you're paying your respects to Smokey in Capitan, check out Oso Grill.

Oso Grill, 100 Lincoln Ave., Capitan, New Mexico, (575)354-2327

Offering certified New Mexico beef and home of the state's best Green Chile Cheeseburger in 2018.

MESILLA

If you find yourself in **Mesilla** and fancy Mexican cuisine:

La Posta De Mesilla Restaurant & Cantina, 2410 Calle de San Albino, (575)524-3524 (laposta-demesilla.com)

Dating back to the 1850s, when it was a stop on the Butterfield Stagecoach Line, it serves the best Mexican food in town. And that's saying something.

In **Ruidoso**, NM (about a half hour southwest of Lincoln):

The Ranchers Steak & Seafood Restaurant, 2823 Sudderth Dr., Ruidoso, NM, (575)257-7540 (therancherssteakhouse/facebook.com)

Decent steak, but closes early (9:00 pm).

ROSWELL

(Yes, that Roswell, about an hour east of Lincoln)
Cowboy Café, 1120 E. 2nd St., Roswell, New Mexico, (575)622-6363 (thecowboycafe.com)

Small but cozy spot open for lunch and dinner. Start your day off right with the chicken fried bacon and gravy.

WHERE CAN I HANG MY HAT AND PUT MY BOOTS UNDER A BED?

Wortley Hotel, 585 Calle la Placita, Lincoln, New Mexico, (575)6534300 (wortleyhotel.com)

The historic hotel, once partly owned by Pat Garrett, is still open for business. It's about what you'd expect in the middle of nowhere, but the dining room does serve alcohol.

The Dolan House B&B, 826 la Placita, Lincoln, New Mexico, (575)6534670 (thedolanhouse.com)

Located right in the middle of town, it also serves lunch.

RUIDOSO

Burned Well Guest Ranch, 399 Chesser Rd., Roswell, New Mexico (866)729-0974 (burntwellguestranch.com)

Its working cattle ranch offers different packages depending on your interests. Check out their website.

WHAT SHOULD I WATCH AND READ BEFORE I HIT THE TRAIL?

BOOKS

- *Billy the Kid: A Short and Violent Life* (1989 by Robert M. Utley)—the authoritative biography of the Kid
- *To Hell on a Fast Horse: The Untold Story of Billy the Kid and Pat Garrett* (2010 by Mark Lee Gardner)—exploring the odd but historic relationship between Billy and his lawman killer
- *The Lincoln County War: A Documentary History* (1992 by Frederick Nolan)—a thorough examination of the violent and corrupt history of Lincoln County, stocked with interesting photographs

VIDEOS

- *Chisum* (1970)—John Wayne is the title character fighting the Lincoln County War with assistance from the Kid. Historically, it's a mess, but it does have the Duke.
- *Pat Garrett and Billy the Kid* (1973)—Noted director Sam Peckinpah's last Western, with the always cool James Coburn as Garrett and country singer/songwriter Kris Kristofferson as the Kid. Look closely and you'll spot Bob Dylan in the mix.
- *Young Guns* (1988)—Brat Packer Emilio Estevez is pretty good as a brash, youthful Kid.

TIPS FROM THE TRAIL?

The allure of Lincoln is that you can walk through the original buildings as they were in 1880. You can definitely stay a night in historic lodgings. But a better plan might be a day trip from Las Cruces, where you can enjoy the nightlife of Las Cruces and Old Mesilla.

A weekend in August, the Friends of Historic Lincoln sponsor 'Old Lincoln Days', featuring a parade, living history demonstrations, and, of course, a reenactment of the Kid's daring escape.

The Strange Murder of Patrick Floyd Jarvis 'Pat' Garrett

Pat Garrett

On the morning of February 29, 1908, the fifty-two-year-old killer of Billy the Kid was riding in a rented buggy along the Mail-Scott Road, a wagon trail that ran east from Las Cruces through Alameda Arroyo. Garrett, accompanied by Wayne Brazel and Carl Adamson, was headed from his ranch west of La Cruces in Bear Canyon back to town, supposedly to finalize the sale of his ranch to Adamson. At approximately 10:30 am, Garrett stepped out of the buggy to answer nature's call, when he was shot in the back of the head by a Winchester.44-40 caliber and finished off by a second blast to the abdomen.

At noon, Adamson and Brazel entered the Dona Ana County Sheriff's Office in Las Cruces, with the latter excitedly proclaiming: "Lock me up! I've just killed Pat Garrett!" That's not the strange part. Brazel was tried for murder, but, after deliberating for a whole fifteen minutes, the jury rendered a not guilty verdict based on Brazel's claim of self-defense. Even considering the notoriously corrupt New Mexico politics of the day, the verdict was shocking. The autopsy report clearly evidenced the slayer of Billy the Kid was in the compromised position of urinating at the time he was shot in the back of the head, although, at trial, Brazel claimed Garrett had drawn a gun on him. Despite the finding of the jury, Brazel's story, simply put, did not make any sense.

There was no shortage of potential suspects who wouldn't have minded seeing the former lawman dead. Brazel was a cowboy for a wealthy rancher who retained an expensive, politically connected attorney, Albert Fall, to defend his employee. Prior to his murder, Garrett was rumored to have been about to bring charges against local ranchers for rustling, and possibly double murder for the death of a local politician, Albert Fountain, and his eight-year-old son. Could Brazel have been a contract killer? The powerful ranchers had been politically opposed to Fountain and had made it apparent they had no interest in seeing a continuing investigation of his killing, which had occurred back in 1896.

Another theory arose that Garrett could have been the victim of an assassin, who was lying in wait along the Alameda Arroyo. A known assassin, 'Killin' Jim Miller, who happened to be the brother-in-law of Adamson, had been seen in the area the day before. Could the planned purchase of Garrett's Bear Canyon ranch be a ruse to lure Garrett to the desolate murder location?

Friends of Garrett attempted to launch an independent investigation, but fundraising efforts petered out (pun intended). The details surrounding the lawman's demise continue to be hotly debated among Wild West enthusiasts and historians, spurring numerous books and articles, and remain the Old West's most famous 'cold case'.

ARIZONA
Tucson
Tombstone
Bisbee
MEXICO
79
10
10
191
191
10
80
19
80
2
2
17

Tombstone

Arizona

Tombstone c. 1881 (Courtesy Arizona Historical Society)

WHAT HAPPENED HERE?

In the late afternoon of October 26, 1881, Deputy US Marshal Virgil Earp and his brothers Wyatt and Morgan, along with John 'Doc' Holliday, walked down Tombstone's Fremont Street to disarm four men suspected of toting firearms in violation of a town ordinance. The suspects, Frank and Tom McLaury and Ike and Billy Clanton belonged to the Cowboys, a band of ranchers known in the area not only for their dubiously acquired cattle but for the hell they rose whenever

Wyatt Earp

172

they came to town. It made sense such a party found itself clashing with the Earps, all of them hardened frontier lawmen. Holliday, a dentist and hard-drinking gambler with a violent temper, was a less likely ally in Tombstone's tug-of-war for law and order. But he was a loyal friend to the Earps, and no stranger to the brothers McLaury and Clanton, so along he went to the vacant lot behind a corral that would become the sight of the Old West's most famous shootout.

Only four years old at the time of the now infamous Gunfight at the O.K. Corral, Tombstone had been rapidly growing since Ed Schieffelin stumbled upon a silver vein in 1877. Upon setting out for his fortune, the fortuitous drifter had been forewarned that all he would find in the hostile Arizona desert was his tombstone. When the time came to name his first silver mine, Schieffelin remembered his detractors and christened his find 'The Tombstone'.

Virgil Earp

The name stuck as word of his silver strike quickly spread, and the sight grew from a silver mine to a boomtown. Within a couple years, Tombstone was a rowdy settlement of over seven-thousand hearty souls, the usual assortment of miners, speculators, gamblers, gunmen, cowboys, and prostitutes, as well as a scattering of legitimate businessmen. In its heyday, it was the largest town between St. Louis and San Francisco.

In December 1879, three imposing men wearing black frock coats and stiff-brimmed hats arrived in town with their wives. James, Virgil, and Wyatt Earp, like everybody else in Tombstone, had come to make their fortunes; another brother, Morgan, would join them the following summer, in July 1880. Wyatt, Virgil, and Morgan all had impressive law enforcement backgrounds—Wyatt, in particular, was renowned throughout the West for cleaning up the notorious Dodge City. So it was only natural for the Earp brothers to supplement their incomes from Tombstone's lucrative saloon business, which included gambling and prostitution, with various lawman positions. Wyatt, in addition to riding shotgun for Wells Fargo, was a Pima County deputy sheriff; Virgil was a deputy US marshal and a town marshal/chief of police for Tombstone; and Morgan was a deputy town marshal. It could be confusing, but in the Western Territories lines separating law enforcement duties and jurisdictions were blurry, at best.

Even before the Earps' arrival, there already existed a strained relationship between the Cowboys and the people of Tombstone.

Decades before miners unearthed silver in the hills of southeast Arizona, ranchers, including the Clanton and McLaury clans, had enjoyed unfettered use of the open range along the San Pedro River, west of Tombstone, and nobody seemed to mind the area's rampant cattle rustling. As Tombstone began to prosper and become more civilized, however, townspeople grew weary of the Cowboys' boisterous shenanigans in town, and of the region's general lawlessness, especially the robbery of the many silver-loaded stagecoaches that left town. Into this tense atmosphere entered the Earps, whose 'heavy-handed' peacekeeping techniques—Wyatt would promptly diffuse an escalating encounter by whacking an unsuspecting aggressor in the skull with the butt of his pistol—soon angered the already disgruntled Cowboys.

Morgan Erap

By 1881, Tombstone was, for all essential purposes, divided into two factions, the Cowboys and the Earps, and the schism was much more complicated than simply white hat versus black. The Earps were in Tombstone to make money, and some of the Cowboys' activities were simply bad for business. By controlling the law in Tombstone, the Earps were also controlling profitable businesses generated from gambling, drinking, and the world's oldest profession. The Cowboys, though, had their fair share of supporters, who considered the Earps overreaching Northern interlopers.

Tensions came to a head on October 25, 1881, the day before the infamous showdown, when Ike Clanton and Tom McLaury rode into Tombstone, each with his own agenda. Tom had cattle business to conduct, while Ike had a drinking spree to orchestrate. He also had a score to settle with Wyatt Earp and Doc Holliday. In a somewhat convoluted set of circumstances, Ike believed

Wyatt had told Doc that Ike had ratted out his fellow Cowboys for a recent stage robbery, a dishonor he could not let slide.

John Henry "Doc" Holliday— the Deadly Dentist.

During the course of the day and evening, while drinking himself into a stupor, Ike managed to argue with and run afoul of both Wyatt and Doc, neither a man to be trifled with. Perhaps surprisingly, Wyatt and Doc let the instances pass and went to bed, while Ike spent the night seething and drinking. When the sun rose, Ike, very much drunk and with a firearm in tow, roamed the streets announcing the impending deaths of the Earps and their volatile dentist friend. Virgil put a quick end (or so he thought) to Ike's dire predictions when he bashed Ike in the skull with his revolver. When Tom McLaury confronted Wyatt about Ike's harsh handling, he swiftly received the same treatment from the unsympathetic lawman.

Virgil dragged Ike before a judge, who fined and promptly released the drunkard. Despite leaving the judge $25 poorer, and with a bandaged head, Ike was nevertheless undeterred and continued brandishing threats, stating all he wanted was 'four feet of ground' on which to fight.

At close to two o'clock, Frank McLaury and Billy Clanton rode into town and met their injured and befuddled brothers at the Grand Hotel. It is still unclear exactly what the Cowboys' intentions were in coming to town armed, but, regardless, the brothers walked down Allen Street to the O.K. Corral and their ill-fated destiny. In the meantime, the Earps and Holliday met at the corner of Fourth and Allen Streets and headed to Fremont Street to disarm the Cowboys. Sheriff John Behan (no friend of the Earps) tried to dissuade the lawmen from confrontation, telling them the Cowboys were unarmed, but his plea fell on deaf ears.

When the Earp posse caught up with the Cowboys, they had assembled at the edge of the vacant lot behind the O.K. Corral, between Camillus Fly's boarding house and photo gallery and the Harwood House, near the corner of Fremont and Third Streets. Virgil Earp immediately confronted the Cowboys, saying, "Boys, throw up your hands. I want your guns." Holliday opened his frock coat and pointed the barrel of a Wells Fargo shotgun at the jumpy

Cowboys. What happened next is not exactly clear, but two shots rang out. Frank McLaury clutched his stomach and staggered into Fremont Street, and Holliday unloaded his shotgun into Tom McLaury's chest. Then all hell broke loose.

For the next century and a half, professional and amateur historians alike would dissect and analyze the ensuing thirty seconds in a futile attempt to trace the path of the approximately thirty rounds that were fired. What is undeniable is that, when the smoke cleared, Tom and Frank McLaury were dead, and Billy Clanton lay dying. Ike, the prime instigator of the inevitable gunplay, promptly scampered for safety when the shooting commenced. Virgil, Morgan, and Doc were all wounded. Only one active participant stood unscathed in the immediately misnamed Gunfight at the O.K Corral: the 'Lion of Tombstone', Wyatt Earp.

In the aftermath, Sheriff Behan attempted to arrest Wyatt, who coolly stated, "I won't be arrested now." Ultimately, Ike Clanton filed murder charges against the Earps and Holliday, who were arrested and even spent a couple weeks in jail. After a month-long preliminary hearing, the Earps and Holliday were exonerated, with Judge Wells Spicer finding the lawmen's actions 'fully justified'. Unfortunately, the judge's decision did not end the saga of the Gunfight at the O.K. Corral.

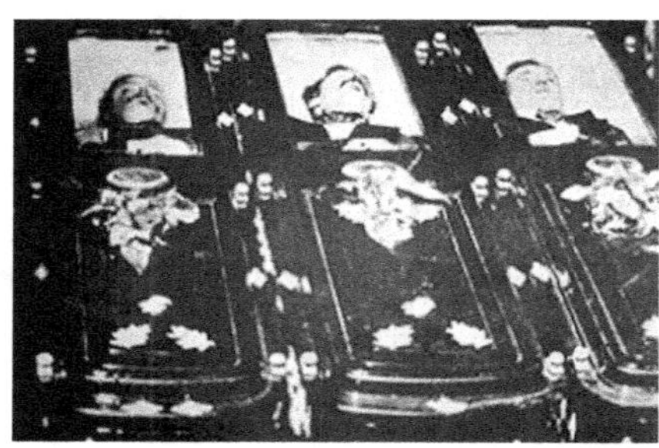

Three dead cowboys, from left, Tom McLaury, Frank McLaury, and Billy Clanton. (courtesy Arizona Historical Society)

On the night of December 28, 1881, Virgil Earp was ambushed as he walked down Allen Street to the Cosmopolitan Hotel. The lawman survived two shotgun blasts but permanently lost the use of his left arm. A few months later, on March 18, 1882, Morgan Earp was murdered by unknown assailants as he played billiards at Campbell and Hatch's Saloon.

The Campbell and Hatch building on Allen Street, was a casualty of the 1882 fire, but was quickly rebuilt. The building is now a Western antique store, that some claim is haunted by Morgan's ghost.

As Wyatt watched the life ebbing from his younger brother, he vowed to track down those responsible. There was no doubt in Wyatt's mind the Cowboys were behind these shootings, and they would pay the ultimate price. Wyatt gathered a posse, which included another brother, Warren, and the ever-faithful Doc Holliday. The group went on what became known as the 'Vendetta Ride'. Under the vague authority of their various law enforcement positions, they scoured Arizona for four months avenging Morgan's murder, leaving in their wake at least a half dozen dead Cowboys, including Curly Bill Brocious and Johnny Ringo. By this time, authorities thought the posse had grown a little too zealous in their peacekeeping duties, and arrest warrants were issued for its members. Wyatt, now a wanted man charged with murder, fled Arizona Territory, bringing an end to the tumultuous period.

The remnants of the O.K. Corral after the 1882 blaze. (courtesy Arizona Historical Society)

Wyatt Earp and Doc Holliday remained friends until Doc succumbed to tuberculosis in Glenwood Springs, Colorado in 1887, at the age of thirty-six. Meanwhile, Ike Clanton, who had managed to elude Earp's 'Vendetta Ride', saw his luck finally run out the same year, when he was shot and killed by a detective. While Wyatt would go on to grow his legend throughout the West, more than four decades would pass before he returned as a curious tourist to Tombstone.

WHAT HAPPENED NEXT?

Tombstone was hit with two devastating fires, one in 1881 a few months before the Earps and the Cowboys clashed, and another shortly thereafter in 1882, both of which wiped out many of the wooden business structures on Allen Street. The mines were still pumping out silver, however, so the resilient inhabitants rebuilt, and the town's boom continued, its population peaking at 20,000 in the mid-1880s.

But bust would eventually follow. The railroad, a key feature of continued progress, never reached Tombstone, foretelling what would become a slow demise, and another fire swept through downtown in 1886, destroying the Continental Hotel; fortunately, the Birdcage theater and Schieffelin Hall were spared. By the 1880s, to access the increasingly elusive silver veins, miners had to

Allen Street

dig deeper and deeper and kept striking water, flooding the deepened tunnels. Expensive pumps were brought in, which ultimately made mining operations cost prohibitive. The town, like the industry that built it, limped along until the last silver mine closed in 1911. Tombstone took another devastating hit in 1929 when the county seat was moved to the copper-mining town of Bisbee.

Shells of buildings on Allen Street circa 1940. (Library of Congress, LC-USF34-036375-D)

'The Town Too Tough to Die' was on life support through the 1940s, when the population dipped to a meager two hundred hearty holdouts, but the popularity of the Western genre in the mid-twentieth century sparked a renewed interest in its historical significance, and an effort was made to increase tourism. Today, Tombstone has approximately 1,500 residents and attracts about a half million tourists a year.

WHAT DO I DO WHEN I GET THERE?

The main drag of Tombstone consists of Allen Street, which runs five blocks, from Fifth Street to First Street. In its heyday, Allen Street stretched twelve blocks, and then, as now, the main commercial area ran along Allen Street from Fifth to Third.
Although there is a visitor's center overflowing with brochures at Fourth and Allen, you don't really need a map to navigate a few blocks. Three blocks of the dirt Allen Street are closed to traffic, and the wooden planked sidewalks are lined with all types of Western shops and saloons.

Looking at the back of the O.K. Corral from Fremont Street.

Stagecoaches run up and down the thoroughfare, and their authentically attired drivers provide paying passengers with colorful insights into Tombstone's violent past. There are, of course, plenty of gunfights to witness, if that's your thing. But beware. In 2015, a gunslinger accidentally used a pistol with live ammunition, resulting in the shooting of a fellow reenactor and the wounding of a stunned tourist. Hate when that happens.

Along Allen Street, there is no shortage of Wyatt Earps, Doc Holliday, and dance-hall girls roping tourists in to watch a gunfight, have a picture taken, or go on a ghost tour. Touristy? Kitschy? A little over the top? Perhaps. But Tombstone is the real deal. Wyatt Earp and Doc Holliday, and other Wild West legends like Bat Masterson and Wild Bill Hickok, all walked these same streets, and enough of the old boomtown still survives to make it worth the trip.

The O.K Corral Historic Complex, 326 East Allen Street (okcorral.com)

Obviously, the main attraction is the O.K. Corral. You enter on Allen Street, and for $10 you walk through the obligatory gift shop and into the vacant lot of what once was the O.K. Corral, which backs into Fremont Street. Access to Fremont from the O.K. Corral is now walled off, so it is difficult to visualize the 1881 gunfight, which actually spilled into Fremont Street.

Allen Street

In order to take you back in time to that fateful day, eight armed mannequins hold the participants' locations, and one even shakes its arm into position to fire off a shot. Disney World it's not, but you are nevertheless treading on the ground where at least part of the bloody showdown transpired.

On the site sits a replica of C.S. Fly's photo studio, which had been located nearby at the time of the gunfight. Fly had been a photographer of some note, and samples of his work are displayed, including old Tombstone photos and compelling images of the Apache leader Geronimo, who once terrorized the area's settlers. Scattered throughout the

The O.K. Corral's lifelike mannequins.

back lot are authentic artifacts from the late nineteenth century, such as wagons, saddles, and buggies, along with replicas of a prostitution crib and even an outhouse.

It wouldn't be the O.K. Corral without a gunfight, so the iconic shootout is performed in front of a Hollywood-type backdrop three times daily. What the thirty-minute show lacks in historical accuracy it more than makes up for with the enthusiasm of the gunfighters. The performers will gladly pose for family photos (tips accepted) after the reenactment. Try not to get shot.

The fee for the O.K. Corral, and the gunfight, also includes admission to Tombstone's Historama, which is adjacent to the O.K. Corral gift shop. A twenty-four-minute film, narrated by Vincent Price (yes, it's that old), explores the history of Tombstone through 'modern' times.

The Tombstone Epitaph, 11 S. Fifth Street (tombstoneepitaph.com)

Your ticket to the O.K. Corral gunfight also gets you into the office of the old newspaper, which still publishes monthly editions. It is no longer located in the original building, but this one dates back to 1895. The office showcases various printing presses and nineteenth-century furniture.

Big Cage Theatre

The Bird Cage Theater, 535 E. Allen Street (birdcagetheater.com)

Opening in December 1881, the combination theater, saloon, gambling hall, and brothel dubbed by The New York Times as the 'Wickedest Theater in the West' was open twenty-four hours a day, three hundred and sixty-five days a year. It is now a museum, its final curtain has dropped in 1889, which is probably the last time it was cleaned. Although jam-packed with artifacts from its heyday, it has to be the filthiest museum in the West. For a not insignificant fee, you squeeze yourself through three cluttered floors of diverse, haphazardly placed Western artifacts, which include such varied items as a faro table linked to Doc Holliday, a funeral carriage used to transport the dearly departed to Boot Hill, a barber's chair, and props from the 1993 film Tombstone. That being said, inside some of the glass display cases, you can find some unique treasures (if you can see through the grime), such as Bat Masterson's cane and a stirrup from his saddle. It is the original building, complete with over one hundred and forty bullet holes, though, which makes it worth the price of admission.

Tombstone Courthouse State Historic Park, 223 E. Toughnut Street

The state park consists of the preserved 1882 Cochise County Courthouse, which is now a wonderful museum. The two-story Victorian building is packed with memorabilia and images telling the history of the mining boomtown and Cochise County. In 2017, the courthouse became the depository of handwritten notes and photos of the Earps, and a typed manuscript by Earp's biographer, John H. Flood Jr., which he compiled during interviews with Wyatt and his common-law wife, Josie, in their later years. As an added bonus, the courtyard contains replica gallows marking the spot when seven men met their maker.

Good Enough Mine Tour, 501 E. Toughnut Street

Wearing plastic mining helmets, tourists are escorted down a steep flight of wooden stairs into the main tunnel of a once-prosperous silver mine. Knowledgeable and humorous guides (okay, maybe they're a little corny) describe the mining process and the life of a miner as they shepherd you

Good Enough Mine

through a series of tunnels. It's not for the claustrophobic, but it is a lot cooler down in the mine than in the scorching summer heat of Allen Street.

Boot Hill Graveyard, 408 Arizona Hwy 80

Despite the gift shop, this is not a tourist trap. It was established in 1879, at the top of a hill, at the end of Fremont Street, as Tombstone's first city cemetery. Among its permanent residents are the victims of the gunfight at the O.K. Corral: Billy Clanton and Tom and Frank McLaury.

IS THERE ANYTHING ELSE?

Tucson is about an hour and a half west of Tombstone on Interstate 10. The Tucson Train Depot, located downtown, is the scene of the slaying of the first victim of Wyatt Earp's 'Vendetta Ride'. Life-sized statues of Wyatt and Doc Holliday memorialize the killing of Cowboy Frank Stilwell.

Old Tucson Studios, 201 S. Kinney Rd., Tucson, AZ 85735, (520)883-0100

The movie studio where hundreds of Westerns were filmed, including John Wayne and Clint Eastwood classics. A lot of the original sets were destroyed in a 1995 fire, but enough still remains to bring back fond cinematic memories. There's plenty of Western film memorabilia, along with gunfights and stunt shows. A great place to visit if you're a Western film buff.

Bisbee, Arizona is located about thirty minutes south of Tombstone. The one-time cooper-and silver-mining settlement is now a quirky, artsy town. The Cooper Queen Mine Tour and the Bisbee Mining and Historical Museum give visitors a glimpse of what mining was like in the nineteenth century.

Fort Bowie National Historic Site is located about an hour and a half east of Tombstone, near Wilcox. Built in the middle of Chiricahua Apache Country, the preserved remnants of the fort are accessible by walking a mile and a half, along the old Butterfield Trail.

WHERE CAN I WET MY WHISTLE?

Big Nose Kates

Although Tombstone doesn't have quite as many saloons as it did when the Earps and Doc Holliday roamed its streets, there are still plenty of venues that allow the thirsty traveler to tip a few in fine Western style. Part of the allure of Tombstone is the opportunity to hang out in a loud, boisterous Western saloon and mix with dance-hall girls, eccentric locals, and fellow tourists. Here are a couple of must-dos:

Big Nose Kates, 17 E. Allen Street (bignosekatestombstone.com)

Named after Tombstone's first prostitute and one-time paramour of Doc Holliday, this lively saloon sits on the site of the former Grand Hotel, which opened in 1880. The original structure did not survive the 1882 fire, but, luckily, the bar did, which means you can belly up to the same wooden slab where Western legends like the Earps, Doc Holliday, and Bat Masterson were served, or overserved as was often the case.

The Crystal Palace, 436 E. Allen Street (crystalpalacesaloon.com)

Originally, the Golden Eagle Brewing Company, the 1880 building was also a casualty of the 1882 fire. It was promptly rebuilt the same year and renamed The Crystal Palace. Over the decades, the structure has housed such diverse commercial establishments as a Greyhound Lines bus depot and a movie theater. Thankfully, in 1964, the Crystal

The Crystal Palace. Virgil was slain in the street in front of this building.

Palace returned to what it was destined to be and now provides a raucous atmosphere for thirsty tourists and locals alike.

WHAT ABOUT GRUB?

The Longhorn Restaurant, 501 E. Allen Street (thelonghornrestaurant.com)

The steakhouse is the oldest continually operated restaurant in Tombstone. In 1880, the location was home to the Bucket of Blood Saloon, and on December 29, 1881, Virgil Earp was ambushed from the upstairs window. In the early twentieth century, the Owl Cafe and Tourist Hotel called the spot home, but it burned down in 1942. The structure was rebuilt in the 1950s and has been the Longhorn Restaurant since the 1970s. It's a step up from saloon fare, and the portions are generous.

The O.K. Café, 220 E. Allen Street (tombstone.org/ok-cafe/)

Open from 7:00 am to 2:00 pm, it's a great breakfast spot with a diner-like atmosphere.

Cafe Margarita, 131 S. 5th Street (cafe-margarita.com/)

Originally the Russ House, a boarding house owned by 'The Angel of Tombstone', Nellie Cashman, the restaurant offers a somewhat diverse menu featuring Mexican and Italian cuisine. Stick with the Mexican. The homey courtyard patio is a relaxing oasis to get away from the bustling saloon scene and enjoy a specialty margarita.

WHERE CAN I HANG MY HAT AND PUT MY BOOTS UNDER A BED?

There may be nicer hotels outside the historic district, but if you're going to be in Tombstone, you really want to park the car and hoof it (especially if you want to play Doc Holliday for the night). There are a couple of motels on Fremont Street that are functional (three-star tops) but clean with accommodating staff.

- Larian Motel, 410 E. Fremont Street, (520)457-2272 (tombstonemotels.com)
- Budget Host Inn, 502 E. Fremont Street, (502)457-3478 (budgethost.com)
- Landmark Lookout Lodge, 781 AZ-80, (520)457-2223 (LookoutLodgeAZ.com)
- Monument Guest Ranch, 895 West Monument Rd., Tombstone, (520)457-7729 (tombstonebmonumentrranch.com)

WHAT SHOULD I WATCH AND READ BEFORE I HIT THE TRAIL?

BOOKS

- *Wyatt Earp: Frontier Marshal* (1931, by Stuart N. Lake)—this popular biography published two years after Wyatt's death is largely responsible for the lasting image of Wyatt Earp as the quintessential Western lawman. With information based on Lake's interviews with the elderly Earp, all of its claims may not stand up to historical scrutiny, but the work influenced generations of writers and filmmakers.

- *Inventing Wyatt Earp: His Life and Many Legends* (1998, by Allen Barra)—an easy read detailing the adventures of Wyatt and the emergence of his image in popular culture as the stoic lawman.

- *Doc Holliday: The Life and Legend* (2006, by Gary L. Roberts)—a compelling look at the sometimes-overlooked dentist turned gambler and his tumultuous travels through the boomtowns of the Old West.

- *Bob Boze Bell's Classic Gunfights, Volume 2, The Twenty-Five Gunfights Behind the O.K. Corral* (2005, by Bob Boze Bell)—richly illustrated look at some lesser-known Tombstone gunfights. Don't worry. He didn't forget the big one.

- *Tombstone: The Earp Brothers, Doc Holliday, and The Vendetta Ride from Hell* (2020, by Tom Clavin)—although there are plenty of books on the West's most famous shootout, Clavin's smooth writing style makes for an enjoyable and informative read.

VIDEOS

- *My Darling Clementine* (1946)—a romanticized account of the showdown at the O.K. Corral. This film leaves no doubt as to who wore the white hats. From a historical perspective, it's a mess, but iconic director John Ford can get away with that. It's still worth a watch.

- *Gunfight at the O.K. Corral* (1957)—big-name stars of the 50s (Burt Lancaster, Kirk Douglas) dominate the screen in this action-packed

Western that culminates in a historically inaccurate but nonetheless entertaining old-fashioned gunfight.

- *Tombstone* (1993)—its history is pretty accurate, and it employs a great cast—Kurt Russell is Wyatt, while Bill Paxton and Sam Elliot play his brothers—but Val Kilmer as the charming yet alcoholic and menacing Doc Holliday steals every scene. You must watch it before you go to Tombstone.
- *Wyatt Earp* (1994)—leave it to Hollywood to go decades without making a Western about Tombstone and the Earps then release two within a year. Kevin Costner's epic three-hour film is well done and also has an entertaining portrayal of Doc by Dennis Quaid.

TIPS FROM THE TRAIL

Every year, starting in 1929, Tombstone has hosted 'Helldorado Days' (tombstonehelldoradodays.com), a weekend celebration of the founding of Tombstone. Usually held on the third weekend in October, the event features gunfights, parades, fashion shows, street performers, and even a carnival.

To Tombstone's credit, a noticeable effort has been made to restore the historic buildings as authentically as possible. The people of Tombstone are friendly and genuinely dedicated to preserving the memory of, arguably, the Old West's most famous town. If the locals make a few bucks along the way, so be it. Just go with it, and soak it all in. You can definitely spend a couple nights here.

The Third and Final Mrs. Wyatt Earp

Old West marriages were not necessarily formalized by civil authorities, who, out on the frontier, were often unavailable to sanction the nuptials. Sometimes, the participants just didn't feel the need to bother with what they perceived as bureaucratic paperwork. The couple simply started holding themselves as husband and wife. Wyatt Earp was no stranger to such arrangements.

Wyatt's first wife, Urilla, died in 1870 after less than a year of marriage. When Wyatt arrived in Tombstone in 1879, he was accompanied by his second wife, Celia Ann 'Mattie' Blaylock. However, the lawman would soon become smitten with a buxom twenty-two-year-old, Josephine Sarah 'Sadie' Marcus. Sadie, the daughter of Jewish immigrants, had started her adventurous life in the slums of Manhattan's Lower East Side. As a teenager, Sadie had traveled West working as an actress, and possibly a soiled dove as well.

By the time the fetching Sadie hit Tombstone, she was the common-law wife of the sheriff, Johnny Behan. The romantic rivalry between Behan and Earp, and political opponents, added kerosene to the already smoldering fire in Tombstone. Decades after the climactic gunfight, Sadie would recall that, as the gun smoke cleared, she ran past Behan and embraced Wyatt, thankful that her one true love was still alive.

Shortly after the shootout, Wyatt placed Mattie, who was slowly sinking into an opium addiction, on a train to Compton, California, to be with his family members. He never saw her again. Abandoned by Wyatt, Mattie's demons increased, and she died from a laudanum and alcohol overdose in 1888.

Upon completion of Wyatt's 'Vendetta Ride', he reunited with Sadie in San Francisco. The pair, although they would never formally marry, would remain dedicated to each other for the next half-century, traveling to boomtowns throughout the West, and

Josephine Srah Marcus. 1881, taken by noted Tombstone photographer C.S. Fly

even to Alaska. The childless couple eventually settled in Los Angles, where Wyatt passed away in 1929 at the age of eighty. Sadie would spend the rest of her life actively participating in the development of publications and films that featured Wyatt as the sanitized, vigilant Western lawman. Sadie would live until 1944, and her remains are buried next to her beloved Wyatt's in Hills of Eternity cemetery, a Jewish cemetery in Colma, California.

90
SOUTH DAKOTA
18
385
18
Wounded Knee
Chadron
Fort Robinson State Park
20
20
385
2
NEBRASKA
26

Wounded Knee, Lakota Pine Ridge Indian Reservation

South Dakota

The Opening of the Fight at Wounded Knee by Fredric
Remington, 1890 (Library of Congress, LC-USZ62-89867)

WHAT HAPPENED HERE?

On the unseasonably mild morning of December 29, 1890, near Wounded Knee Creek in South Dakota, members of the legendary 7th Cavalry, none other than George Armstrong Custer's former regiment, attempted to disarm a Sioux band as they made their way to the Pine Ridge reservation. Things went horribly wrong. What ignited the impending disaster is still unclear, but a shot was fired from the Indian camp, prompting soldiers to unleash an awesome amount of firepower on the unsuspecting Sioux. When the smoke cleared, the last significant engagement between the US Army and the Indians was over, leaving as many as three hundred Sioux dead, many of them women and children.

Earlier that year, the US Census Bureau had declared the American frontier closed. However, the conflict between this small band of ragged and tired

Sioux and the men of the 7th Cavalry would prove the government bureaucrats wrong, even before the calendar could turn a new leaf over.

By the mid-1880s, the government's policy had been to 'divide and conquer' the various Native American tribes, and to confine them to small, separate reservations. The tactic was successful, and by 1888 most of the Plains Indians had been forced onto government reservations. The proud, nomadic Sioux were now dependent on often corrupt Indian agents to ration food and other necessities. In 1889, the degrading drudgery of reservation life was suddenly disrupted with the reemergence of an Indian spiritual ceremony called the Ghost Dance, which started to spread among the various tribes across the West (see p. 203). The ritualistic dance was peaceful; it promised that the living Indians would be reunited with their dead ancestors and that the white man would perish from the Earth, leaving the Indians alone to enjoy the Earth's bounty in peace.

The Ghost Dance

Despite the symbolic nature of the ritual—even the most superstitious government and military leaders surely realized dead Indians rising from their graves was a long shot—the US government became deeply concerned. It feared the Ghost Dance would be a vehicle to unite the tribes it had just spent a couple of decades trying to separate. White settlers in towns and ranches located close to reservations were also getting panicky and demanding that something be done, so the Bureau of Indians Affairs (BIA) banned the Ghost Dance and requested the Army restore order to the Sioux reservations.

It is understandable why the defeated Sioux would have embraced a religion that promised them a better life. What is not as understandable is how the government and white settlers could have realistically believed a peaceful religious movement posed such a threat that forceful military action was necessary. In any event, tensions and fears among the whites continued to escalate through 1890, reaching a feverish pitch on December 15, 1890, when Sitting Bull, the legendary Sioux medicine man, who by then had been suspected of becoming involved with the Ghost Dance movement, was killed during his arrest at Standing Rock reservation. After Sitting Bull's death, hundreds of his followers left the Hunkpapa Sioux camps at Standing Rock and began traveling almost two hundred miles south to the Pine Ridge reservation to meet up with the highly regarded Chief Red Cloud and the Oglala Sioux.

One of the bands traveling through harsh winter conditions to Pine Ridge was led by Miniconjou Sioux Chief Spotted Elk (commonly known as Big Foot for the size of his moccasins), whose followers comprised a few hundred men, women, and children. The already arduous journey got off to a bad start when Big Foot fell seriously ill with pneumonia.

The different Sioux bands leaving their designated reservations and joining together is exactly what the Army didn't want to happen, which is why Gen. Nelson A. Miles gave Col. James W. Forsyth and his 7th Cavalry the clearest of orders: "Disarm the Indians. Take every precaution to prevent their escape. If they choose to fight, destroy them."

Gen, Nelson Miles

Col. James Forsyth

Big Foot and his ragged band managed to evade the Army for a couple of weeks, but on December 28, members of the 7th Cavalry finally caught up with the Miniconjou Sioux near Wounded Knee Creek, about eighteen miles from the headquarters of the Pine Ridge reservation. Under a flag of truce, Big Foot was assured the tribe would be escorted unharmed to Pine Ridge the following morning. Arrangements were even made to transport the ailing Big Foot by wagon. That night, the weary and unsuspecting Sioux set up their tipis by Wounded Knee Creek, not far from where the 7th Cavalry bivouacked. In front of his tent, Big Foot conspicuously posted a white cloth, signaling peace, and awaited the morning.

At daybreak on December 29, 1890, four hundred mounted soldiers under the command of Col. Forsyth approached the camp and ordered the Indians to surrender their weapons, which they reluctantly stacked before the suspicious soldiers. This half-hearted surrender of armaments led the soldiers to suspect the Sioux had not turned over all their guns, and so a search of the tipis commenced.

Things quickly escalated when one Indian, Black Coyote, would not hand over his weapon, a shiny new Winchester. Whether he refused to do so because of outright disobedience, his fondness for the weapon, or because he was deaf and simply unable to hear the order was never determined. He would not live to tell his side of the story.

Chief Big Foot (Library of Congress, LC-USZ62-116812)

As the tense confrontation with Black Coyote played out, a medicine man started performing a Ghost Dance and throwing dirt into the air, which likely spooked the undertrained cavalrymen. Suddenly, a shot rang out, possibly from Black Coyote's prized weapon, and all hell broke loose. Forsyth was not about to make the same mistake as his predecessor Custer; he did not leave the big guns behind. Trained on three sides of the Lakota camp were four multi-barrel rapid-fire Hotchkiss guns. Upon hearing the shot, the jittery soldiers immediately opened fire, indiscriminately mowing down not only the unarmed Sioux but also their fellow soldiers.

Chief Big Foot was among the first to fall. In a blanket of smoke, the vulnerable Indians scattered in all directions, vainly seeking some kind of shelter. The fleeing Indians were no match for the mounted Cavalrymen, who caught up in the frenzy, relentlessly chased down the Sioux, sometimes for miles, and slaughtered them all, even the women and children.

One survivor later recalled: "There was a woman with an infant in her arms who was killed as she almost touched the flag of truce… A mother was shot down with her infant; the child not knowing that its mother was dead, was still missing…. The women as they were fleeing with their babies were killed together, shot right through… and after most of all of them had been killed a cry was made that all those who were not killed or wounded should come forth and they would be safe. Little boys… came out of their places of refuge, and as soon as they came in sight a number of soldiers surrounded them and butchered them there."

After the massacre, unrelenting snow fell on frozen ground for the next three days, blanketing the dead and dying. On New Year's Day 1891, a civilian contactor burial party uncovered the frozen corpses and, a few days later, unceremoniously dumped them in a mass grave at the top of a hill. Prior to the mass internment, the soldiers, as a final show of disrespect, perhaps in retribution for the indignities perpetrated on their fallen comrades-in-arms fourteen years earlier on the grassy slopes of the Little Big Horn River, stripped and looted the lifeless bodies for souvenirs.

The warrior survivors were enraged and determined to exact revenge. The next day, about fifteen miles north at White Clay Creek, the Sioux were able to pin down the 7th Cavalry, who had to be rescued by the buffalo soldiers of the 9th Cavalry. But the sporadic attacks soon died out, and the deflated Sioux begrudgingly accepted the inevitable and returned to the reservations.

Initial reports noted that the 7th Cavalry had performed admirably and that the battle would be 'a wholesome lesson to the other Sioux'. Twenty of the 7th Cavalry's soldiers would be awarded the country's highest military decoration, the Medal of Honor. However, Gen. Miles soon started to have his doubts as to Col. Forsyth's claimed 'victory'. The 7th Cavalry, with four hundred well-armed soldiers, had vastly outnumbered the Indian camp's approximately three hundred members, the majority of whom were unarmed women and children. Why then were there so many casualties?

Burial of the Dead (Library of Congress, LC-USZ62-44458)

The 7th had lost twenty-five men, and thirty-three were wounded. The Indian dead were numbered at a hundred fifty-three, but that figure was believed to be inaccurate since it was surmised that relatives had removed a large number of the dead.

Big Foot's Camp three weeks after Wounded Knee Massacre. (Library of Congress, LC-USZ62-46006)

It was also suspected the Army had removed some of the most devasting evidence of the atrocity before the arrival of the burial party. Why were more people killed than in any prior encounter with the Indians, except for the Little Big Horn debacle a decade and a half before? Why was it necessary to kill so many women and children? Officially, Gen. Miles relieved Col. Forsyth of command and ordered a court of inquiry to examine Forsyth's tactical decisions. In particular, Miles questioned whether Forsyth's positioning troops on all four sides of Big Foot's camp had led to the unnecessary loss of life by 'friendly fire'. Privately, Miles had no doubt as to Forsyth's perceived incompetence, writing to his wife, Mary (niece of Lt. Gen. William T. Sherman), "Forsyth's actions [are] about the worst I have ever known," and the result was 'the most abominable military blunder and a horrible massacre of women and children'.

The final chapter of the Indian Wars had come to a horrific and sad conclusion, ending almost four centuries of conflict between westward-bound Americans and the Indigenous peoples.

WHAT HAPPENED NEXT?

A military court of inquiry was quickly convened, a move that upset many within the officer corps, who were appalled that the quick decisions made by a commander in the field were being scrutinized. Additionally, Forsyth was a well-respected Civil War veteran, rising during that conflict to be Gen. Phil Sheridan's chief-of-staff.

The court exonerated Forsyth, and as noted by *The New York Times*, he was 'restored to command of his gallant regiment'. Forsyth retired as a brigadier general in 1897.

The US Army regarded the massacre as the last victory of the Indian Wars, and glorification of the atrocity would continue for years. In 1914, Buffalo Bill Cody, the old scout turned showman, produced and starred in a moving picture called The Indian Wars, which included a 'reenactment' of the Wounded Knee battle. The filming took place at the actual location and featured a seventy-four-year-old Gen. Nelson Miles.

The Box Office Bust—The Indian Wars

Needless to say, the filmed version of the battle painted the 7th Cavalry in a heroic light, which justifiably outraged the Lakota Sioux who were cast in the movie.

Predictably, the movie flopped at the box office, a failure that ended Buffalo Bill's movie career.

Periodically, pressure has been put on Congress to make amends to the Sioux for the massacre. It took until 1903 for the Wounded Knee Surveyors Association to able to erect a monument on the site of the mass grave in memory of those who perished that December morning. In 1917, and again in 1920, with the assistance of Gen. Miles, Congress was asked "to atone in part for the cruel and unjustifiable massacre of Indian men and innocent women and Wars. Children at Wounded Knee."

The 1920 inquiry concluded with a proposal that the Lakotas be compensated twenty thousand dollars for property stolen off the frozen cadavers left on the massacre site; no action was ever taken. In 1938, Congress introduced a bill to compensate the heirs of those killed with a thousand dollars, but the bill died on the House floor. In 1965, the battlefield was finally designated a national historic site, but in 1968 forty acres of the Pine Ridge Indian Reservation, including the massacre site, was privately acquired by allotment, a system by which the federal government divided reservations into smaller parcels for sale. The white owner who purchased it lived on the property and established a trading post and museum.

In 1973, about two hundred Sioux, led by members of the American Indian Movement (AIM), a militant political and civil rights organization that had also occupied Alcatraz Island in San Francisco Bay from November 1969 to

June 1971, claiming native peoples had the right to the former federal prison under a treaty provision granting to Indians unused federal land forcibly occupied the small town of Wounded Knee to protest police brutality and prejudicial government policies. Consequently, federal and state law enforcement personnel quickly responded and surrounded the site. Gunfire was exchanged, and, after a seventy-one-day siege that left two Sioux men dead, the activists left the property, but not before burning all the buildings to the ground. The trading post and museum were never rebuilt. Today, there is a small Wounded Knee Museum in Wall, South Dakota.

In 1990, a hundred years too late, Congress issued a formal apology to the descendants of the victims of the massacre but, once again, stopped short of awarding reparations or providing funds for a national monument. As recently as 2019, a bill was wheeling its way through Congress that, if passed, would rescind the twenty Medals of Honor awarded to the 7th Cavalry soldiers for their actions at Wounded Knee. Also, in 2019, a plan to open a museum in Rapid City, South Dakota showcasing Medal of Honor recipients was kiboshed because the Wounded Knee awardees would be among the honorees.

Today, the Pine Ridge Indian Reservation consists of approximately 2.1 million acres in southwest South Dakota, on the Nebraska border, and is home to approximately twenty-five thousand members of the Oglala Sioux Tribe. The three counties that encompass the reservation are among the poorest in the United States, and alcoholism, drug abuse, and depression remain continuing problems among tribal members. Incredibly, many of the homes lack electricity and running water.

The actual massacre site remains in private hands, and the forty acres, landlocked by tribal land, were put up for sale in 2013 for close to four million dollars. The sale included neither Sacred Heart Church nor the Wounded Knee Memorial, which the federal government gave to churches for their mission work on reservations, so, technically nobody owns it. The cemetery, meanwhile, is maintained by the Wounded Knee Survivors Association. Through the years, the price has been lowered but is still not close to the million-dollar range, which the Oglala Sioux Tribe feels is a fair price, despite a market value, setting aside the site's historical significance, of less than ten thousand dollars. The Sioux has expressed an interest in purchasing the property and creating a holocaust memorial and museum, but, as of now, the price remains too high.

Because of the 1890 massacre, and the bloody occupation in 1973, Wounded Knee remains a symbol to many of both the atrocities committed by the US government against Native Americans and of Native American activism. Every year since 1986, the Big Foot Memorial Riders make the thirteen-day trek on horseback from Big Foot's camp to Wounded Knee to help ensure Americans never forget the tragedy that happened there.

WHAT DO I DO WHEN I GET THERE?

Wounded Knee Massacre Monument, BIA Hwy 28, Wounded Knee, SD 57794

Wounded Knee Memorial

It truly is a somber, desolate place. Driving on Highway 28, looking, mostly in vain, for directional signs, the telltale indications of poverty hit you right in the face: dilapidated trailers, heaps of assorted junk, and trashed cars.

Upon arriving at the monument, you face a big red sign that informs you of the horror that occurred there on December 29, 1890. On my visit, on a fittingly freezing cold October afternoon, as my companion and I read the sign, out of the corner of my eye, I saw a cloud of dust spread across the horizon. No, it was not a herd of horses but a beat-up, blue and green 1990s vintage Cadillac with no license plates racing toward us. The Caddy stopped with a screech and out-jumped two young Native American women selling various handmade jewelry and crafts—dream catchers, bracelets, earrings. If you read reviews on Yelp or TravelAdvisor, the presence of these entrepreneurs, and of men wanting to give unofficial tours (something I didn't experience), is a common complaint.

Welcoming Sign

Some visitors say they feel intimidated by their presence, although I did not. I only felt sad. Sure, the company of these independent vendors is a little distracting, perhaps even an intrusion on an otherwise solemn site, but the whole thing is mostly depressing, a tangible reminder of the necessity of tourism dollars to a proud people long oppressed and still suffering under its yoke. Perhaps some perspective is required by all.

Beyond the red sign and the wooden kiosks set up to sell crafts, lie the killing fields of Big Foot's encampment. Up a gravel road is the cemetery, the final resting place of those carelessly tossed into the mass grave. The graves and the 1903 monument are enclosed by a cyclone fence, which is haphazardly yet reverently adorned with wreaths, ribbons, and rags.

There is no museum, no Visitor Center, and no bathrooms, but the somber experience is nonetheless one a visitor cannot forget. In some ways, the eeriness and bleakness of the site are appropriate. You come face to face with the stark reality that the US Army killed hundreds of unarmed Indians, including a large number of women and children. It's a historical fact, and the cold, hard evidence is right in front of you. In taking in your surroundings, you have no choice but to confront the reasons why, in the twenty-first century, Native Americans still live in abject poverty on reservations.

I am cognizant the tone of this chapter is uncharacteristically subdued. The venture to Wounded Knee is not your typical tourist experience, but it is a vital part of the history of the Old West. We should never forget the westward expansion of the United States, the fulfillment of Manifest Destiny, came at a price. Some paid more than others, and some are still paying. Every American should pay their respects at Wounded Knee.

IS THERE ANYTHING ELSE?

Fort Robinson State Park, 3200 Hwy 20, Crawford, NE 69339-0392, (305)665-2900

Crazy Horse Death site

About an hour and a half southwest of Wounded Knee, Fort Robinson was an active military post from 1874 to 1948. The twenty-two thousand-acre state park offers hundreds of miles of hiking, biking, and horseback-riding trails. Some of the historic military quarters have been converted to overnight guest lodging. On May 6, 1877, the feared Crazy Horse rode into Fort Robinson with close to nine hundred Lakota followers and finally surrendered, marking the end of The Great Sioux War. Crazy Horse made a poor adjustment to life on the reservation, and within a few months had managed to run afoul of both Army leadership and jealous tribal leaders, a conflict that culminated in his

Ft. Robinson

fatal bayoneting by an Army sentry during a scuffle outside the Fort guardhouse on September 5, 1877.

Crazy Horse's father, Worm, buried the enigmatic warrior somewhere in the Pine Ridge country of Dakota Territory, but the exact location, somewhat fittingly, remains a mystery.

A rough carved stone in front of the replica guardhouse marks the spot of Crazy Horse's fatal stabbing.

WHERE CAN I WET MY WHISTLE?

The Favorite Bar, 155 Main Street, Chadron, Nebraska, (308)432-5366

Favorite Bar

Located halfway between Wounded Knee and Fort Robinson is the small former fur trading town of Chadron, Nebraska, home to The Favorite Bar. It is the definition of a dive bar. The beer is cheap and cold, and the clientele, a group known to liberally drop F-bombs with abandon, is colorful but nevertheless friendly.

WHAT ABOUT GRUB?

77 Long Branch Saloon, 115 Main St., Chadron, Nebraska, (308)432-3380

Located in the Old Main Street Inn. Has decent steak and a pretty good bar.

**The Ridge, 164 Main Street, Chadron, Favorite Bar
Nebraska, (308)747-2255**

Serves basic American fare in a bar-type setting.

WHERE CAN I HANG MY HAT AND PUT MY BOOTS UNDER A BED?

Holiday Inn Express & Suites, 247 Ash St., Chadron, Nebraska, (877)834-3613

The free breakfast bar is key.

Olde Main Street Inn, 115 Main Street, Chadron, Nebraska, (308)432-3380

Pretty good B&B in a building listed on the National Register of Historic Places.

WHAT SHOULD I WATCH AND READ BEFORE I HIT THE TRAIL?

BOOKS

- *Bury My Heart at Wounded Knee: An Indian History of the American West* (1970, by Dee Brown)
- *American Carnage: Wounded Knee, 1890* (2014, by Jerome A. Greene)—detailed analysis of the military operation that led to the debacle

VIDEOS

- *Bury My Heart a Wounded Knee* (2007, HBO)—a fairly accurate TV movie adapting the last two chapters of Dee Brown's masterpiece

TIPS FROM THE TRAIL

GPS is very spotty, and directional signs are hard to come by, so look at a good old-fashioned map before you go. Go with the right attitude. It's not a touristy, fun place. Don't be put off by the locals attempting to sell their crafts. They mean no harm and are just trying to get by. Maybe buy something while you're there. It's the least we can do.

The Ghost Dance

During a solar eclipse on January 1, 1889, a Paiute medicine man in Nevada named Wovoka (aka Jack Wilson) had a vision that the messiah had returned to Earth to save the Indians. The spiritual leader, who claimed he could levitate and catch bullets, foresaw that all white men would disappear, the buffalo would return, and, most miraculously of all, the Indians would be reunited with their dead ancestors.

Wovoka (National Archives)

The path to this new white-free world was a ritualistic performance called the Ghost Dance. Although based on older round dances performed by Indians, the Ghost Dance had some special characteristics. First, participants had to be purified through fasting and sweat baths, and their faces had to be painted. An integral part of the Ghost Dance was the required attire, muslin shirts, and dresses painted with special symbols, such as crows and eagle feathers, known as Ghost Dance Shirts, which would protect them from harm, including bullets fired by the US Army. The Ghost Dance was a five-day-long ceremony in which the believers would dance every night, and all night on the fifth night, finally working themselves into a frenzy.

Wovoka's teachings, which were peaceful, soon spread to other tribes, who enthusiastically embraced the Ghost Dance until it became a bonified religious movement within the tribes.

As the Ghost Dance spread throughout reservations, officials in the federal government became alarmed, while some White Americans argued it was essentially harmless, a legitimate exercise of religious freedom.

Others in the government saw malicious intent. The practice was seen, in a way, to energize and unite Indians against White rule. By late 1890, authorities in Washington began giving orders for the US Army to be ready to take action to suppress the Ghost Dance, a decision that culminated in the deadly confrontation at Wounded Knee.

After the Wounded Knee Massacre, it became tragically apparent to the Sioux that the Ghost Dance Shirt did not have magical protective qualities, and the Ghost Dance movement lost all its momentum and most of its followers. Although the red sign at the memorial inaccurately states that "Ghost Dancing ended with this encounter," the ritual continued elsewhere on the plains, though to a limited extent. A Sioux tribe in Canada continued to practice the Ghost Dance into the 1960s. Wovoka also would keep his faith in the Ghost Dance until his death in 1932, at the age of seventy-four.

Index